The Reliant Robin

The
Reliant
Robin

Britain's Most Bizarre Car

Giles Chapman

The
History
Press

First published 2016

The History Press
The Mill, Brimscombe Port
Stroud, Gloucestershire, GL5 2QG
www.thehistorypress.co.uk

British Library Cataloguing in Publication Data.
A catalogue record for this book is available from the British
Library.

ISBN 978 0 7509 6759 4

Typesetting and origination by The History Press
Printed in China

Cover illustrations: *Front*: The Robin 850. *Back, from top*: Graphic from the Robin van brochure; The Robin LX.

Frontispiece: The proud author and his new purchase.

Right: The handbook, plus all the cash found under the seats!

Contents

Acknowledgements

I am greatly indebted to the following people, who very generously gave their time and knowledge to help me get things right in this book, and to add their valuable insight and/or support:

Ken Akrill of Keygate Motors (keygatemotors@talktalk.net / 01634 841279)

Annabel Chapman (apologies for the grumpy days)

Ian Fuggle

Tom Karen, former head of Ogle Design

Nick Kisch

Joe Mason of Reliant Spares (www.reliantspares.com / 07973 470810)

Elvis Payne (www.reliant.website)

Alexander Scheidweiler

Herman Tandberg, design director, Ogle Noor Ltd

Paul Taylor

Chris Thomas

Iain Wakefield, Haynes Publishing

All illustrations are from my own collection, unless otherwise stated.

Introduction

Within a few days of this book first being suggested, I became a Reliant Robin owner myself. You know how it is; the moment something crosses your mind, you turn to the Internet to see how the land lies. I'm very familiar with the world of escalating classic car prices, but I was incredulous at the bidding activity for Reliant Robins on the auction website eBay.

No matter what state of decrepitude the cars were in, people were chasing them with zeal. Even complete wrecks were well into three figures, while scruffy but functioning cars had twenty or more bids, and were changing hands for thousands of pounds.

Zipping around online, the reason for the frenzy soon became obvious. As of 2015, just 1,840 Robins of all types were left, according to reliable, official DVLA statistics of Britain's registered vehicles. That's out of a surprisingly large total of more than 63,000 cars made. The Robin is often called a British motoring institution, but clearly it's not one the country has valued highly: until, perhaps, now. And with prices for excellent examples of 1950s European bubble cars like Isettas and Messerschmitts sometimes reaching a dizzying £30,000, a Robin at under £2,000 has to be a fantastic investment opportunity.

It is, after all, Britain's most famous three-wheeler – a unique machine that, throughout its twenty-seven years on sale, never had a rival that was even remotely as successful. Moreover, it has cult British 'designer' provenance. The cheeky and instantly recognisable outline of the original Robin, believe it or not, hails from the very same design studio that brought you the Bush TR82 portable radio, the Chopper bicycle, the Popemobile and even the Landspeeder from *Star Wars*.

Not that I paid anything like £2,000 for mine. There it was for sale on a small ad website, Gumtree, with the only photo showing it buried under mountains of junk in a lock-up garage in Chessington, Surrey. A mere £150 was being asked, but there were plenty of catches: no keys; documents lost as relatives shovelled through the late owner's effects; no word on whether it was working. It also had a tight deadline for collection: before noon on Friday, or the council was going to destroy it when they took back possession of the house and lock-up garage.

It wasn't even the actual, original, flat-fronted, round-eyed version of the infamous plastic pig that I really desired, but one of the later Robin hatchbacks. And it was a Thursday afternoon.

By 10 a.m. on Friday, I found myself on the M25, in the passenger seat of a recovery vehicle, hauling it home.

My wife was not best pleased. As it rolled down the truck's ramp, the steering locked, and for two weeks it sat resolutely unmovable outside our house. It is social suicide in suburbia to have a Reliant Robin on your drive. Eventually, I managed to clear enough space in my garage and, with a friend, bounced it around on the single front wheel until we could roll it in.

Since then, I've been pondering my design 'classic' in all its vile blue glory (the paint colour is like a medical waste sack from a hospital, not exactly complemented by orange go-faster stripes). Some time very soon I'm going to get it working but, meanwhile, it has at least been saved for posterity.

As a car, it's not good. The flimsiness of just about everything on it is positively unnerving. By even the most basic standards of modern motoring – indeed, even compared to the typical metal-bodied, four-wheeled family car of the mid 1970s – the Reliant is gapingly inadequate. Could it ever have been worth the penny-pinching of a tiny fuel thirst, motorbike road tax and a 25 per cent reduction in tyre consumption to risk your neck on Britain's roads – thronged with impatient truck drivers and risk-taking, teenage daredevils – in one of these manifestly unstable, motorised margarine tubs?

That one is very hard to answer. The Robin, from a twenty-first-century perspective, is a product well out of its time. The environment and society in which Reliant built up its extraordinarily loyal following is today another country entirely.

Throughout the 1950s and '60s, its three-wheelers were a singular phenomenon in Britain's automotive industry – a bridgehead between true microcars, with their generally motorbike-derived twin-cylinder engines, and 'proper' cars, with four cylinders and reasonably civilised accommodation. It was produced by a firm with an ethos like no other, and which ploughed the money it made from selling three-wheeled vehicles into a quadruple life as a sports car company, a supplier of ready-made car industries to developing countries, and a leading position in the technology of that itchy stuff that used to lag the nation's lofts – glassfibre.

The Robin first appeared in 1973, and the timing simply couldn't have been better. The world, the UK included, was about to be plunged into a deep recession, as war in the Middle East strangled oil supplies. Petrol prices soared and everyone was looking for ways to make their precious allocation go further. For a time, the stylish little car from Tamworth was just the thing, and Reliant dealers were taking in hundreds of 'real' cars in part exchange.

Yet the years to come proved difficult for the Robin to navigate. The chill winds of justified mistrust blew it off course and 1980s prosperity melted class divides and widened aspirations; for a while, the avian name itself was a burden and was temporarily changed. The Robin shuffled towards its belated demise in 2001, at which point seeing one on the road was still nothing unusual. In the intervening period, though, these tricycles for grown-ups have dwindled rapidly. If you're out on the high street with your young children and a Robin drives past, they'll stare, shout, point and ask questions.

In fact, I've found plenty of adults are also intrigued by the Reliant Robin and its place in Britain's motoring zeitgeist. How, they wonder, did anything like that – anything so willfully eccentric – ever get to be a credible mode of transport in the modern world? Well, read on …

One

Tom and Raleigh

The Reliant Robin first emerged for public scrutiny in 1973 as a brand-new car, but it could already lay claim to a heritage stretching back over forty years, and very few people had any inkling that its roots were with Britain's most famous brand of bicycle.

The Raleigh Cycle Company came into being in 1888 and expanded hugely and rapidly as the Victorian craze for cycling burned red hot. By 1913, it was said to occupy the world's largest bike factory in Nottingham, at which point it had already enjoyed a brief dalliance with another newfangled invention, the motorbike, which Raleigh also manufactured for around six years. For a brief time, between 1903 and 1908, if offered the Raleighette, a three-wheeled motorised tricycle; the single wheel was at the back and two passengers could be crammed into a basket seat between the front wheels as the rider controlled the vehicle from behind. The word deathtrap springs to mind ('forecar' was the official title) and, not surprisigly, there weren't many takers.

After that, Raleigh stuck doggedly to pedal power, and it was only after the First World War, in 1921, that motorcycle manufacture resumed. Powered two-wheelers seemed a natural extension to the firm's main business, and by that time it had a network of 400 dealers who could sell its motorbikes too.

Always looking for ways to keep the noses of the workforce at its vast factory pressed to their grindstones, in 1930 Raleigh acquired the rights from a friendly rival motorbike firm to a strange, three-wheeled

Tom Williams, Reliant founder, with the naked chassis of a Regal MkVI in February 1962. (Elvis Payne)

delivery vehicle called an Ivy Karryall. It was obviously based on a motorcycle design because there were handlebars and levers for throttle and brakes, and the driver sat on a saddle astride the banging single-cylinder engine, which took power to the back axle via chains.

With a few modifications, the vehicle was relaunched as the Raleigh 5cwt Light Delivery Van, which offered a thrifty commercial vehicle for small businesses, perfect for local deliveries, at a rock-bottom price.

Almost simultaneously with this, Raleigh recruited a new chief designer, 41-year-old Tom Lawrence Williams, hailing from Tamworth in Staffordshire, who had built himself a solid reputation designing Triumph and then Dunelt motorbikes. Just about the first thing he did was to improve the little Raleigh van, changing the magneto to coil ignition and the levers to foot pedals, adding shock absorbers to the rear suspension and fitting better lights and windscreen.

The prototype of the Reliant van at a picturesque stop during an assessment by *Commercial Motor* magazine in 1935. (Elvis Payne)

Many think this crude contraption was the working Reliant prototype, when in fact it was a cut-down van given a BSA engine and put to work on a farm. (Elvis Payne)

A fine period image of a 1950 Reliant 10cwt van, showing the motorcycle-like 'girder forks' sticking out of the box-like body that were characteristic of this little workhorse. (Elvis Payne)

The Austin Seven, one of the most popular pre-war British cars, provided the 747cc four-cylinder engine for 500 Reliants in the late 1930s.

The contraption was still super cheap, at a paltry 75 guineas. Williams upgraded it again two years later, distancing it even further from its motorbike roots by devising a clever steering system that now included a proper steering wheel and a seat for the driver, which could be swung out of the way so that the little vehicle could be kick-started! The price crept up to £87, but there were still plenty of takers.

Next Raleigh decided, or else Williams convinced them, to create a proper three-wheeled family car, which they called the Safety Seven. Three-wheelers for carrying people rather than crates and boxes weren't a new idea – BSA, Coventry Victor and Morgan had been making them for years, but they all had the single wheel at the back. Raleigh's smart little four-seater car, because it used a version of the van chassis, had the single wheel out front.

However, it was much more pokey, being gifted a JAP 742cc V-twin engine from supplier JA Prestwich Ltd and a three-speed-plus-reverse gearbox sending the drive via a shaft to the rear axle. The suspension was underslung at the back, giving the Safety Seven a ground-hugging

Motorbike/sidecar 'combinations' were a stepping stone for riders when it came to providing a small family with transport, although no doubt the missus wasn't always pleased with the discomfort and noise.

attitude that resulted in safe handling and, considering its modest power, pretty good stability. When all the planets of weather and gradient were aligned properly, the little car could manage 50mph. It had an eager nature, which was demonstrated on the 1934 Land's End Trial, where it romped up the punishing hill sections with gusto. Plus it looked no less modern than contemporaries from large manufacturers.

It sold well, with 3,000 examples shifted between 1933 and 1936. The very fact, though, that it was axed without being replaced pointed to Raleigh's indecision about its motor-vehicle division. It was planning to float on the stock market in 1936, where its position as a world-leading bicycle maker was its best calling card.

Tom Williams started to feel uneasy about his future with the company. He was convinced there was a good market for the three-wheeled Light Delivery Van, and he decided in summer 1934 to exploit it himself if Raleigh didn't want to. He set up a workshop in the back garden of his house, Bro Dawel, on Kettlebrook Road, Tamworth, and with an ex-Raleigh colleague called Ewart 'Tommo' Thompson they built their own prototype, mostly by hand but with bits of assistance from local garages. Classic entrepreneurial stuff. There was no animosity from Raleigh. Actually, the Nottingham company was happy to sell the two industry hopefuls as many components as they needed for their vehicle, as they hand-fabricated the chassis and installed a 600cc V-twin JAP engine.

Many of the Raleigh parts were stamped with a prominent capital 'R', which probably helped steer Williams into picking the name Reliant for his new enterprise. The early part of 1935 was extremely hectic. The prototype was road-registered on 1 January, and in February Tom had signed the lease on a disused Midland Red bus garage at Watling Street, Two Gates, Tamworth for use as a factory. It may have looked unpromising at the time, but it was destined to be the centre of the Reliant universe for the next sixty-four years. The Reliant

A rakish Swallow sidecar made by the ancestor of Jaguar in the 1920s and '30s, and the transport for many an uncomplaining girlfriend of young bloods. Fun while they lasted.

Engineering Company Limited was formed on 1 April, with a share capital of £5,000. There was solid support for Tom's venture from Mr W.J. Bennion, the manager of the local branch of Barclays Bank, which led to a very long-lasting relationship.

The first of the £84, 7cwt vans was delivered to its new owner on 3 June 1935. Sales were a bit slow at first but the rudimentary production line in the draughty old bus depot slowly built up production to one and then two examples each day of this 'New Form Of Transport', as they called it. With plenty of challenges, small and large, along the way, Reliant was up and running.

Two

Vans and Bonds

The Reliant van was an odd-looking beast: a box on wheels with what looked like the front forks, wheel, mudguard and single headlamp of a motorbike jutting out of the front of it. It would never be the sort of vehicle in which you'd like to see your daughter travel on her wedding day. But for Britain's legions of one-man bands and small businesses in the late 1930s, it was just the ticket: cheap to buy, thrifty to run and – despite the basic nature of its specification – very manoeuvrable around town.

There was plenty of room for improvement, though, and Tom Williams was restless in his quest for a better product.

A longer chassis meant that in 1936 he could offer a version capable of carrying 10cwt of cargo. This came with a more civilised engine, a 747cc water-cooled JAP twin-cylinder, where the drive was taken via the three-speed-and-reverse gearbox to the back axle. The driver now sat on the right-hand side of the cramped little cab – although there was no passenger seat – and there were various other detail improvements for the new £106 price tag.

Smooth running it certainly wasn't, and in 1937 Tom Williams made a leap of imagination that would define Reliants from that point on. He struck a deal with Austin, one of the biggest car companies in the UK, for 500 four-cylinder engines from the world-famous Austin 7. It was fitted into beefier 8- and 12cwt Reliant vans, and the passenger car refinement it offered with its four pots instead of two was a revelation, even though the actual capacity was identical at 747cc.

The downside was that the bigger engine intruded into the passenger compartment and a special kinked gearlever was needed to make the thing comfortable to use.

No sooner had manufacture of the new vans begun than Austin decided to stop making the 7 altogether. Maybe they'd seen Tom coming, but it was a hammer blow for the ambitious Tamworth firm. The boss would not be bowed. He took the extraordinary decision to make his own engine, and in six weeks had created a close copy of Austin's unit. What's more, he and his chaps designed all the tooling and jigs necessary to make the engines in house. Of course, there were teething problems aplenty, but by the time the Second World War began in earnest, Reliant had built eighty of its vans with its very own engine in a factory which it now owned outright. It was a remarkable leap to near-total self-sufficiency for such a shoestring enterprise. Reliant was now master of its own, tiny destiny.

The vans were quickly back in production in 1946, the factory now bristling with new machine tools acquired during the war in which Reliant had played a big part, turning out some 1.5 million machine parts for the mechanised offensive against the enemy. In 1950, the 12cwt was replaced by the fully revised 10cwt Regent van, with a host of updates. The most significant were the proper doors with sliding windows that made daily delivery life in bad weather just that bit less dispiriting, and the hydraulic shock absorbers that genuinely enhanced the van's ride comfort.

Kellogg's CORN FLAKES

BOND MINICAR

No. 28 in a Series of 40 Cards.

This model is the world's cheapest and most economical family car. Giving over 100 miles to the gallon, the Bond Minicar cruises at 35–40 miles an hour, and has a maximum of 45. It is powered with a single cylinder two stroke engine of 122 c.c. Constructed chiefly of light alloys, the total weight of the car is only 310 lbs. Accommodation is ample for 2 adults and a child, with a large luggage boot at the rear.

Look out for your favourite model

COLLECT THE SET—
save 'em; swop 'em.

BOND MINICAR

The Bond Minicar in its original MkA form featured on a collector's card given away with Kellogg's Corn Flakes. It offered stability, weather protection and stupendous economy at a rock-bottom price, and probably inspired the first Reliant passenger car.

The company was really into its stride, and would go on to make some 7,000 Regent vans by 1956, which at about forty a week meant the factory was truly bustling. In 1954, too, an elongated body, with an opening front bonnet and even a mascot featuring three circles inside a chrome comet, appeared on the Regent Mk2, doing its best to conceal the motorbike-like front forks. It was, just about, a proper van that any business could be reasonably proud of.

So with this solid business, and a ready market, why would Reliant want to get involved in the tricky business of selling passenger cars to consumers?

The vans were certainly workaday products, stripped of all fripperies to keep the price low, and every customer wanted it that way. They would always do okay in their own rut, but times were changing. By 1950, many of the austere, post-war government-imposed restrictions on petrol and the new-car market had been lifted, unleashing a tidal wave of demand for the latest family cars.

New models of small car like the Morris Minor, Austin A30, Ford Popular, Standard Eight and Hillman Minx were snapped up as fast as their factories could turn them out. Further up the scale there was even more choice, with the new Standard Vanguard, Ford Consul, Austin A40 Somerset and Vauxhall Wyvern/Velox jostling for attention.

Right at the bottom of the scale, though, there was something else – something really new. In 1948, the three-wheeled Bond Minicar had arrived. It was an absolutely minuscule vehicle, its single wheel at the front powered, if that was the right word, by a single-cylinder, two-stroke 122cc Villiers engine more normally found in a small motorcycle. As it was mostly constructed from aluminium, and lacked even such basics as opening doors (you jumped in), rear suspension (the air in the tyres took on that task) or a glass windscreen (it was Perspex and wouldn't stay free of scratches for very long), the first Minicar weighed just 310lb. No need for a reverse gear; you could lift it up at one end to back it into a tight parking space.

This Ford Popular was pretty much the most basic new car you could buy in the early 1950s, and economical too, but Reliant reckoned it could out-thrift even this austere little beast.

The very first Reliant Regal offered little in the way of frills, although a nuclear family of four could just about squeeze into its boxy contours.

The RELIANT "REGAL"
DE LUXE MODEL
Lowest priced FAMILY MOTORING
ON THREE WHEELS
50 MILES TO THE GALLON
65 MILES PER HOUR

An early Regal MkII brochure extolling the tempting cocktail of miserly petrol consumption and fairly spritely performance, with a little added glamour thrown in.

What kind of a freak would want one of these? Well, at just £242 in 1950 for the 197cc Deluxe edition, it was very cheap indeed. But there were two pulls that were even more alluring than that. The first was its tiny appetite for fuel. Okay, so it wouldn't go much faster than 40mph, but 75mpg was easily possible. And, if you drove it in timid district nurse mode, you could eke out a gallon of petrol over an astonishing 100 miles. The second was that, weighing a lot less than the official upper unladen weight limit of 8cwt – 895lb in the Imperial measures of the day, or 406kg by today's metric measures – the little Bond was legally classified as a tricycle. As such, anybody only in possession of a motorbike licence could drive it, which meant that you could have a 'car' with rudimentary protection from weather and injury – steered by a wheel and not handlebars, with a driving seat rather than a saddle, and pedal-operated accelerator, brake and clutch – without the inconvenience or expense of taking your full car driving test.

Admittedly, it doesn't sound like much of an advantage in the twenty-first century. Remember, though, that the 1940s was an era of deprivation and rationing. The working classes may have been gifted the Welfare State, with its National Health Service, council house building programme and decent education for all, but money was very tight.

Moreover, there was a vast army of working men, everyday people earning their living through hard graft, who aspired to something better in life. Ever since the dawn of the twentieth century, a sort of travel pecking order had grown up that was constantly in flux.

If you walked to work at the shop, factory, mine or steelworks then you aimed one day soon to be able to cycle there. If you biked there then you envied the relative lack of effort involved on a motorbike. A motorbike, of course, was all right if you were on your own; your

No equivalent Car can offer so much

★ Up to the minute styling.
★ Comfortable four seater.
★ Economy — 50 m.p.g.
★ Performance — 65 m.p.h.

★ 4 cylinder water-cooled engine.
★ Hydraulic brakes on all wheels.
★ Tubeless tyres.

This inner page of a brochure for the Regal MkIII shows the glass-fibre hardtop that, for the first time, turned the car into a snug family saloon ready to hold its head up high in suburbia.

The chassis illustration from the Regal MkIII brochure amply demonstrates the problems of the engine position when it comes to 'packaging' the car for its occupants.

Fresh air wasn't denied to Regal acolytes in the drophead version of the MkIII, although this would prove to be the final open-topped Reliant.

Close competition for three-wheeler custom came constantly from Bond with its evolving Minicar. This press advertisement for the MkC was from Raymond Way Motors, the country's biggest distributor.

girlfriend might not mind riding pillion, but once you were married then you might have to get a sidecar. However, even in the late 1930s, the ultimate final leap in personal mobility to a second-hand car was still beyond most blue-collar workers.

The Bond Minicar made a serious attempt to break down this barrier. It was, just about, a car, and although the purchase price might have been a stretch for many, the extreme economy it offered meant it was no more costly to run than a small motorcycle.

This whole scenario cannot have evaded Tom Williams and his colleagues. His own workforce, after all, was typical of small factories all over the land: hard working, hard pressed and keen to improve their lot in life.

Yet, Tom could see a gaping chasm in the market for a 'hybrid' three-wheeler, one that could benefit from the legal concessions that tricycles enjoyed, yet offer a rather more grown-up driving experience that was closer to that of a real car and was a quantum leap away

RELIANT

MAKE YOUR FAMILY SELF-RELIANT

Who takes your children to school? Who carries home that heavy shopping? Your wife, no doubt, but not in your car. Give her a second thought, buy a second car that will do 50 miles per gallon, cruise at 50 m.p.h. and yet costs only £5 per year in Tax. Very safe to drive and easy for parking. This is real motoring economy. This is the Reliant Regal Mk.111.

your second Car

50 miles per gallon
£5 Annual Tax
Low Insurance

London Distributor:
Glanfield Lawrence (Highbury) Ltd.
Reliant House, 28-32 Highbury Corner, London, N.5.

RELIANT ENGINEERING CO. (TAMWORTH) LTD.
TWO GATES, TAMWORTH, STAFFS.

RELIANT "REGAL" Mk.III.

Persuasive advertising began to pitch the Regal MkIII as an ideal second car – anticipating future British consumer trends. Chances were, if you could run to a second car, a Reliant wouldn't really have been your list topper, but nice try.

The Bond Minicar tried to shed its image of absolute minimalism in the MkC by sprouting fake wings/mudguards to bring the tiny headlights into the main body.

from the crudity of machines like the Bond Minicar and the similarly compromised Villers-engined AC Petite.

From Reliant's viewpoint, there was potentially a lot more profit to be made from selling cars to the public rather than tight-wad, small tradesmen, and there was no reason why the company couldn't sustain both car and commercial vehicle clienteles. Plus, don't forget, Tom Williams was no stranger to cars, having been the brains behind the moderately successful Raleigh Safety Seven in the mid 1930s.

So, throughout 1951, the Reliant crew worked flat out on the prototype for a passenger car and the results were exhibited at the Motor & Cycle Show at London's Earls Court in early November. They called it the Reliant Regal 4-Seater Coupe, but no actual price was yet quoted.

Although the chassis was derived from the one underpinning the trusty Regent, it was all new for the car, with a welded box-section frame in which the familiar Reliant engine and gearbox were fitted set well back from the front. Ahead of the power unit was the most fundamental change. The old motorbike forks had gone and an all-new front suspension system was provided, consisting of a forged leading arm pivoted at the back and with a kingpin at the front end to facilitate the steering mechanism and hold the single wheel's stub axle in position. A horizontal torsion bar was fixed to the chassis at one end. It was

'You owe it to yourself to have a free trial run'; Bond Minicar MkC advertising trumped the Regal MkIII for mpg while trailing it for mph.

Cover artwork of the Bond MkC brochure, somewhat expressing the lack of concern for child safety in those carefree motoring days.

a neat, quite elegant engineering solution, although old-fashioned half-elliptic springs remained at the back supporting the 'live' axle.

The engine might have been in the optimum position for stability, but it made a big imposition on cabin space and to do any work on it you didn't lift the car's stubby bonnet (under which were the battery, radiator and, in the prototype, the fuel tank) but unfastened a cowling between the narrow driver's and passenger's footwells to access the engine from inside the car.

The bodywork consisted of aluminium panels fixed around an ash-wood frame. The car was a convertible, so there was a hood and detachable side screens, but the rear seat was really only big enough for children, and there was no boot.

As to the outward appearance of the Regal, it could, at best, be described as plain; professional-looking by the standards of most trikes, but ugly, its slab-sidedness made all the more box-like by the

A dramatic demonstration of glassfibre's lightweight advantage over metal, as the inner plastic structure of the pioneering 1953 Chevrolet Corvette is held aloft.

rectangular nose of the vehicle, with its single front wheel tucked well inside. The prototype looked well-turned-out, yet it had one serious handicap: it was too heavy to be classified as a tricycle in the UK.

So in the months ahead, as prototypes embarked on a vigorous road-testing programme, a rethink was needed. Manufacture of the Regal in its original form got underway for export markets where the weight restriction wasn't a problem, but the company brainstormed on ways to make its new baby slip neatly inside the 8cwt weight bracket. The key move was to shrink its dimensions; the wheelbase was shortened by 10in, length by 13in, width by 4.5in and height by 2.5in. They also swapped glass side windows for plastic ones. While they were in the mood for change, they moved the petrol tank to the back, provided boot space that was accessible via a folding back seat, and positioned the spare wheel under the bonnet.

It was in this much revised and generally shrunken form that the car hit the UK market in January 1953. The price was a mere £362 including purchase tax and, in the year of the queen's coronation, there was great play on the Regal name. Even in those days, it was extremely basic transport, likely to have no appeal to someone used to the sophistication, lavishness and spaciousness of, say, a Morris Minor. But thanks to Tom Williams and his team, it was the new king of three-wheelers – powerful enough not to get left behind in the cut and thrust of daily traffic, relatively refined, and with all-round economy paramount. Everything else with three wheels was motorbike-powered, but the Reliant had a proper car engine and a young family could just about be squeezed on board.

After a slow start, the public were really keen on it. Some 154 cars were sold in 1953 and another 855 the following year, up to the point when the MkII arrived, which had an improved driving position and a final drive ratio on the axle reduced from 5.4:1 to 5.1:1 for better performance and economy. There was also a modest price increase to £403. Customers would clearly have loved a saloon model to keep Britain's driving rain and wind at bay, but making one out of metal would have certainly pushed the weight up beyond that crucial 8cwt level.

However, the cutting edge of high technology was about to make its impact on Reliant. Glass-reinforced plastic, also known as glass fibre, was a new wonder product that had huge potential as a lightweight material in car construction. Over in the USA, the entire body of the Chevrolet Corvette sports car was made of it, and in the UK Jensen

Reliant's Regal MkIV was the first to have a roof section moulded into the body and it also featured a proper opening boot lid. Getting very like a 'real' car now.

was an unlikely pioneer of it on its handsome 541. With the gaffer Tom Williams and company sales director Tom Scott fully behind the move, Reliant decided to get in on the act.

Its first use was in the roof and side panels of a new MkII Regal van priced at £353 and, once the company had got to grips with moulding techniques for the new plastic composite, they turned their attention to the coupe, creating a glass-fibre hardtop that could transform it into a snug little saloon, all for an extra cost of just a tenner.

Really getting into their stride, Reliant started to fit some glass-fibre side panels to its cars in 1955, too. Every unnecessary pound they

As Bond began to feel the competitive heat from the more car-like Reliant Regal, it came up with the full-bodied MkE, which also benefited from a four-speed gearbox.

The BMW Isetta set out to solve the basic transport conundrum in a very different way, with the engine and single wheel at the back and the whole front doubling as the single door.

could shave off the vehicle's basic construction could be added back in improved comfort, and, boy, did the cars need that.

So there was much excitement in 1956 around the Regal MkIII – the first Reliant to have a body made entirely of glass-fibre panels, albeit one still relying on an ash frame as its inner structure. There was still a choice of open or hardtop models, but the convertibles fell out of favour as most buyers plumped for the comfort of a roof. Reliant had had problems trying to mould a bonnet panel that kept its shape, but now, with a wider and more car-like frontage than ever, they took the opportunity to reduce the bonnet to a small hatch panel. Even so, if you planned to do anything to the engine, your best hope was from the cockpit anyway.

There were a couple of things that kept Regal demand extremely buoyant throughout 1956 and '57. First was the generally more attractive lines of the three-wheelers. Plastic moulding meant the body panels didn't have to be kept dead straight any longer to allow minimal panel beating by hand, and so the lines of 'normal' cars were copied for the new Regals, a move that vastly improved their visual appeal.

The other, somewhat more salient, factor was the so-called Suez Crisis – the dwindling supplies and soaring costs of petrol after the British Government, clinging on to its last bit of Imperial strong-arm tactics, tried vainly to wrest back control of the Suez Canal in the face of rising Egyptian nationalism. The aborted venture was a disaster, and Britain soon withdrew, but the effect was to reintroduce petrol rationing. Cars that could make a gallon of juice go as far as possible were now the flavour of the day and Reliants, along with a whole host of tiny-engined 'bubble cars' from Germany and Italy, were the main beneficiaries.

Through the short-lived MkIV (its lighting brighter after an upgrade from a 6-volt to a 12-volt electrical system) and then the longer MkV (with its much-improved rear-seat room, proper boot lid and finally, thank goodness, glass side windows and even a second windscreen wiper), demand was continually increasing. It now looked like quite a substantial car. Indeed, it was the first to have the main body as a one-piece moulding, with the roof an integral part and not a separate add-on. The little fins that Reliant designers stuck on the back gave the very thinnest affinity between the chrome-laden monsters that were then all the rage in the USA and the money-saving trikes peculiar to Britain. But this all had to be compensated for by losing something heavy, and this time it was the spare wheel!

The steering in the Isetta snapped into position once the door was closed. Originally a four-wheeler, a special three-wheeled version was built in Britain to fit local tricycle tax laws.

You might have thought that the arrival in 1959 of that incredible stroke of economy-motoring genius, the Mini, would have truly put the kybosh on Reliant's growth. But not a bit of it. The Regal MkVI appeared in 1961 and, despite only being on sale for two years, a huge 8,478 examples were sold, almost twice as many as the 1959–60 MkV.

On 31 October 1962, Reliant unveiled its most audacious assault yet on the small family car market. Even if you looked down your nose at three-wheelers – as anyone who had tried a Mini, Ford Anglia 105E or Triumph Herald must surely have done – you had to take your hat off to the company's boldness in developing an all-new car with a brand new engine.

First, that engine. There was a real imperative to find a replacement for the existing power unit. It was essentially a 1930s engine hampered with a side-valve design at a time when overhead-valve units were making cars much more responsive. First thoughts centred on a straightforward overhead-valve substitute, but that added a weight penalty of at least 50lb, which immediately ruled it out. Then the project leader Ron Heathcote made the mental leap of imagination to scheme an engine made entirely from lightweight aluminium, in place of the heavy iron previously used for the engine block and cylinder head.

It would be more expensive to make, but eventually the prototype weighed in at just 138lb (62.6kg). Even at a smaller capacity of just 600cc, the new four-cylinder engine, with its crankcase cast as part of its block, was much more lively, and Reliant developed a new aluminium four-speed gearbox to go with it. The motors were installed in MkVI vans and subjected to over 100,000 miles of on-road testing, and in 1960 the all-new powerpack became available in the van. It was one heck of an achievement for an outfit the size of Reliant, and the engine became the first completely light alloy car engine to enter mass production in the UK, easily beating the Hillman Imp's.

Three

Regals and Rebels

The engine was central to the concept of Reliant's 1962 debutante, which, rather than being called the Regal MkVII, came with the title of Regal 3/25, signifying three wheels and the peppy 25bhp of power offered by the new engine. It sat in a lightly revised chassis, with the main difference being a coil spring for the single front wheel instead of a torsion bar.

The body of the new three-wheeler was radical in two ways. Firstly, it pioneered a new construction method that did away with the wooden frame of models past and replaced it with separate inner and outer body mouldings, which, when bonded together, formed a monocoque structure that was then securely bolted as one unit to the steel chassis. The wooden floor of earlier Regals was consigned to history. Not only was it lighter than predecessors but also much more rigid, which not only made the car quieter but also gave a much less flimsy feeling.

And then there was the way it looked. There were any number of design directions that Reliant's stylists could have chosen, but the decision was taken to copy the extremely popular Ford Anglia 105E, with its reverse-rake rear window that gave excellent rear headroom within a short wheelbase where the rear seat was perched atop the back axle. The car was distinctive and practical and also a lot more enjoyable to use, with its wind-down windows, carpeted cover over the gearbox's hump in the cabin, and efficient new heater, which, for the first time, was fed by hot water from the radiator.

The new Regal 3/25 proved to be wildly more popular than earlier cars. By June 1968, production had hit an astounding 50,000, and that was in spite of a serious fire at the factory in December 1965, which took the paint shop, the roof and about £150,000 with it.

But we have to backtrack to 1963 for a couple of important events.

There was a small but significant change in the law that now permitted a reverse gear to be fitted as standard to all tricycles like the Regal 3/25. Until then, every Reliant three-wheeler delivered to the company's dealer network came with a metal plate that shut off reverse gear. If you'd only ever passed your motorbike test, the plate stayed firmly in place, which meant you had zero rearward manoeuvrability, just as you might on a Norton, BSA, Ariel or Matchless two-wheeler. As long as you waved your full car licence under the dealer's nose, the plate could be removed and reverse was yours. It was truly an anachronism, as well as a bind for traffic police to check, and was thankfully done away with.

The other big news for 1963 was the arrival of the Supervan. It was based on the Regal but never shared the name. With its box-shaped back end, 50cu.ft of carrying space and payload of 5cwt, it was practical enough, and boasted a side-opening door allowing unimpeded access. Very much a working vehicle, on the Supervan even a passenger seat was an optional extra.

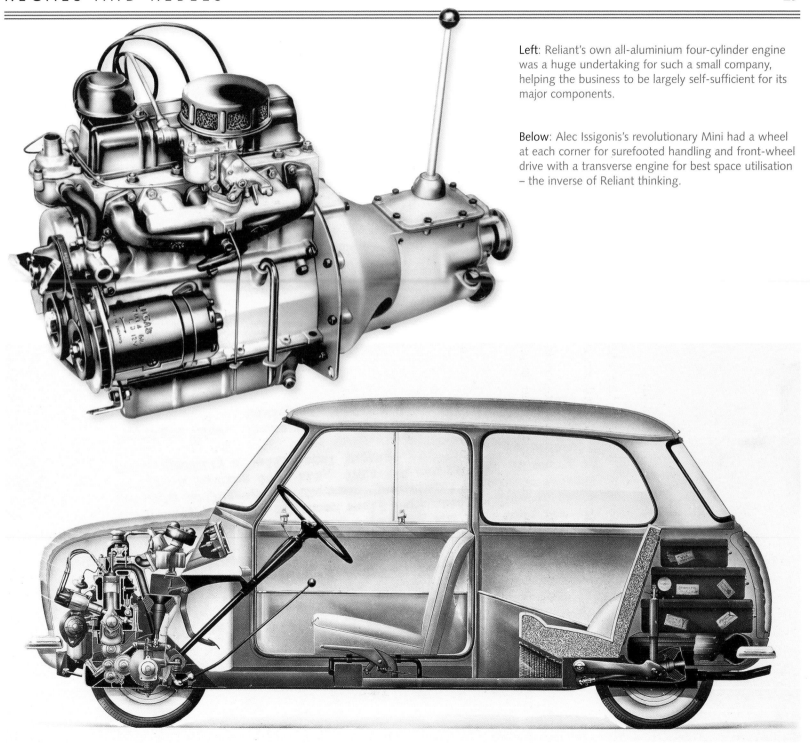

Left: Reliant's own all-aluminium four-cylinder engine was a huge undertaking for such a small company, helping the business to be largely self-sufficient for its major components.

Below: Alec Issigonis's revolutionary Mini had a wheel at each corner for surefooted handling and front-wheel drive with a transverse engine for best space utilisation – the inverse of Reliant thinking.

The world's most famous Supervan – indeed, the world's most famous Reliant – was the one featured in BBC1's *Only Fools And Horses* with (left to right) Uncle Albert (Buster Merryfield), Derek 'Del Boy' Trotter (David Jason) and Rodney Trotter (Nicholas Lyndhurst). (BBC)

BMC's Mini (the one above is a Morris Mini 1000 MkII in 1968) changed the world of small cars forever. Its appeal was classless and its abilities proven in everyday use and on racetracks and rally circuits worldwide.

Above: Here we have the original version of the Regal 3/25, which was new throughout under its sharp-edged, double-skinned body.

Below: The lines of the trendy Anglia 105E – the first British-made Ford to reach 1 million sales – were clearly inspiration for the profile of the Regal 3/25's reverse-rake rear window.

Above: Motorbike champion Cecil Sandford and co-driver David Cooper used this Regal 3/25 to follow (rather than compete in) the Monte Carlo Rally in 1963, showing off the car's stamina.

Left: Autocars took its Reliant-designed range to the USA but imports there sold very poorly, as they were nowhere near as robust as the advertising would have you believe ('sabra' is also an affectionate slang term for a tough, Israeli-born Jew).

Below: The Sussita Station Wagon, a very basic car designed in 1958 to be built in Israel to Reliant designs and exploiting the company expertise for its glass-fibre body.

When its Israeli client Autocars asked for a sports car, Reliant came up with this, the Sabra (named after a local prickly pear cactus), for which it supplied design, engineering and kits containing the parts. The saloon cars in the background are examples of the Autocars' Carmel, another Reliant design.

Reliant decided to manufacture the Sabra for the British market and sell it from 1961 as the Sabre 4, with a 1.7-litre Ford Consul engine; they sold 200 examples, plus another eight cars with this redesigned nose treatment.

The man at the wheel is Boris Forter of Helena Rubinstein. In 1962, the cosmetics tycoon commissioned Ogle Design to build him this one-off car, the SX250, to his personal tastes and specifications.

The Ogle SX250 made a big impression on Reliant's Tom Williams and Ray Wiggin. They bought the design rights, married the car to the old Sabre chassis, fitted a six-cylinder Ford Zephyr engine, and created the Scimitar GT, launched in 1964.

Above: The Scimitar GT was a surprisingly accomplished and fine-handling car, considering its erratic roots, and suddenly the company was a new force in the sporting car business.

Right: Designing four-wheeled cars for assembly abroad led to the launch of the 1964 Rebel, an economy car with a Reliant engine and plastic body. It was a very minor player in the mainstream car market, thanks to intense rivalry from the Mini, Imp, Fiat 500 and 600, and Renault 4.

KEEP DOWN RUNNING COSTS

the money you save is profit you earn

Rebel 750 Van :for a longer working life.

Right from the word go the new Rebel 750 will save you money.

With its 750 cc. engine the Rebel will do up to 45 m.p.g. on a run and carry a full 5 cwt. load plus driver and passenger. And with its hydraulic clutch and all-synchromesh gearbox it will make short work of those round-the-houses deliveries that have been costing you so much time and money.

Like all Reliant cars, the Rebel 750 has a glassfibre body and a sturdy box-section steel chassis. You don't need overnight garages to protect this tough little van. Because the body cannot rust it does not matter if you leave it out in all weathers. And if it's bumped or bashed glassfibre localises damage, cutting repair costs and off-the-road time.

Find out more about the Rebel 750 Long life van.

Reliant Motor Company Limited, Marketing Services Division, Tamworth, Staffordshire. Tel: Tamworth (STD : 0827 4151)

This leaflet tried to promote the Rebel van as the ideal companion to the self-employed tradesman. Once again, the Ford Escort, Morris Minor and Bedford HA vans crushed it underfoot.

Yet another Reliant product returning to the company's workaday roots was the TW9 pickup. These examples are freshly completed at the Greek factory of Mebea, another of Reliant's long-time overseas affiliates.

Local authorities loved the TW9 for its low running costs and the ease with which it could negotiate narrow streets in towns and cities. This pint-size road-sweeper conversion was offered by Melford Engineering and had an additional Reliant engine in the back to power those spinning brushes.

The car industry went GT-mad in the 1960s and the transformative effect was carried out on this Regal 3/25 Super by Middlesex dealer Two Strokes Ltd, with racy matt-black bonnet, 'bullet' racing mirrors and go-faster coachlines.

Above: Hmm, well, it says Special on the number plate, but this dealer-modified Regal 3/25 Super probably just offered a cosmetic makeover to make it stand apart from the crowd.

Left: Interior view of the Regal Super makes the padded rear seat look quite inviting, while the driver's seat, with its stunted backrest, hardly looks to be the most comfortable vantage point for a long trip.

Ogle Design carried out its first assignment for Reliant by restyling the jagged frontage of the Regal 3/25 for this Super version launched in 1965 for £486.

The gritty reality of delivery work in a cramped three-wheeled van is turned to an advantage in this advertising poster for the Supervan, issued in the early 1970s.

There was up to 50cu.ft of cargo space inside a Supervan, making it very useful for local delivery duties; Royal Mail and airline BOAC operated small fleets of similar vehicles.

Reliant's 21E (which stood for 21 extra features) treatment was extended to the Supervan to produce a luxury version of the little chariot.

Spotlights and bright trim were included in the Supervan 21E edition, but the pretty girl, pedigree pooch and light aircraft all had to be paid for separately.

GET UP AND GO... WITH THE NEW RELIANTS

Regal 21E-700 and 3/30 Saloon

The Supervan would become, in the 1980s, the most famous Reliant there's ever been. A battered yellow example was cast alongside David Jason and Nicholas Lyndhurst in the phenomenally popular BBC1 comedy *Only Fools & Horses*. With a little bit of magic from the BBC props department, it was carefully 'distressed' and plastered with the livery of Trotters Independent Traders, famously boasting branches in New York and Paris, as well as Peckham in south-east London.

Anyone who knows anything about Reliants is constantly correcting people who think it is a Reliant Robin (or even, indeed, a Regal) when it isn't. They are 'plonkers' and 'dipsticks' for getting it wrong.

1968 brochure to signal the launch of the Regal 3/30, with a new 700cc engine giving a useful fillip of power for extra taking-off power.

Sheer logic
Seven solid reasons why you can afford a car after all

1 Rising petrol costs: *no problem.*
The Reliant 3-wheeler gives up to 60 m.p.g. or even more. Top speed over 70. Yet there's plenty of room for 4 people and a large boot for their luggage.

2 £25 licence: *no problem.*
To license the Regal costs only £10 a year.

3 HP deposit: *no problem.*
Reliant HP deposit is *pounds* less than for 4-wheel cars. Supervan is free of Purchase Tax too – and down payment could be 25% or less.

4 Rust: *no problem.*
Reliant body and doors are made, not of metal, but of tough, reinforced glass fibre. This is why you never see a rusty-bodied Reliant: why Reliants need no garage. Glass fibre *cannot rust,* ever.

5 Maintenance, repairs: *no problem.*
The engine block is all-aluminium like a Rolls-Royce's; it can handsomely outlast a cast-iron engine. And the body, being glass fibre, minimises the effect of any accident, so repairs are cheaper.

The Regal, weighing under 8 cwt., is also very easy on tyres. Average life is forty *thousand* miles. Only three tyres to replace anyway!

6 Replacing your car: *no problem.*
All cars depreciate but Reliants depreciate less than other cars. This means they command a good re-sale price when you buy your next Reliant.

7 Insurance costs up: *no problem.*
You can insure the Regal for as little as £10 a year, depending on circumstances and type of cover.

No 4th wheel. So? So you're £1.10 a week better off.*

Now is the time to take action

Send this coupon to Rodney Hackett,
Reliant Motor Company, Tamworth, Staffs.
☐ Please send me information about the Reliant Regal four-seater saloon. *List price from £668.2.6. Inc. p. tax.*
☐ Please arrange a road test.
☐ Please send me information about the 5 cwt. Reliant Supervan III. *List price from £506.0.0. No p. tax.*
☐ Please arrange a road test.
Name
Address

RELIANT REGAL
sheer logic

* *Compared with running a small four-wheeled car.*

Above: Ogle Design built this Scimitar GT-based show car – the GTS – for Pilkington to showcase Triplex glass techniques in automotive design; the sporty estate-car profile fed directly into the Ogle/Reliant Scimitar GTE.

Left: A Reliant advert for the Regal, in 3/30 guise, putting the case forward for buying one; pure logic would surely have favoured a four-wheeler, were it not for financial prudence.

Left: In 1968, the glass tailgate of the Scimitar GTE opened up a new world of practicality in sporting cars and would reappear on a certain three-wheeler five years later.

Below: That's not actually Princess Anne at the wheel of this 1971 Scimitar GTE, but she was a very keen owner after receiving one as a twentieth birthday present in 1970.

This angle perfectly shows the accomplished design of the Scimitar GTE, surely one of the greatest ever to come from the drawing board of Ogle's Tom Karen.

On 5 March 1964, Reliant's formerly robust founding father Tom Williams suffered a heart attack at his desk and died shortly afterwards. He was just shy of 74. This Midlands motor industry legend had built his company from scratch and, in his usual forceful way, had carefully laid a plan for succession. Indeed, it was his personally groomed assistant managing director, Ray Wiggin, who drove him home on that fateful day and who stepped smartly into the breach as the new boss after his passing.

The two colleagues had, by this time, developed Reliant into a very unusual company. The three-wheelers provided the bedrock of its activities, with glass-fibre bodies made at a plant in Kettlebrook and engines produced at another one in Shenstone, feeding into the main factory at Two Gates, Tamworth. Having become unusually adept in using glass-fibre for car bodies, from 1958 Reliant lost no time in marketing its expertise. It designed a little four-wheel estate car called the Sussita and helped Israeli firm Autocars to establish a plant to build it. When Autocars said it would like to make a sports car too, Reliant cobbled together a design (Ashley kit-car body, Ballamy chassis, Ford engine) for the Sabra two-seater at minimal cost. When the Haifa operation hit problems, Reliant relaunched the Sabra as the Reliant Sabre 4 roadster in Britain in 1962 and suddenly it was in the sports car business.

Emboldened by what they could achieve on the minimum of resources – after decades of carving out the trike business from nothing – Williams and Wiggin were suddenly hit by the role that good design could play in a new product. When they spotted an uncommonly handsome prototype GT car at the 1962 London Motor Show, they realised that here was a property just ripe for exploitation at minimal cost. The car was a one-off custom created for a car-mad executive in the cosmetics industry; the chassis was from the Daimler SP250 and the bodywork had been styled and built by Ogle Design. The man responsible was one Tom Karen, an urbane Czech product designer now running the Letchworth-based consultancy after the untimely death of founder David Ogle. As well as cars, the company's work was a fixture in many British homes because it designed the Bush TR82 portable radio, a best seller instantly recognisable for its oversized circular dial and exceptionally sleek lines.

Reliant duly acquired the rights to Ogle's design and the Ogle SX250 was transformed into the Reliant Scimitar GT, using the old Sabre chassis but now with a straight-six 2.5-litre engine from the Ford Zephyr MkIII. The year was 1964 and the car would elevate the Reliant name to the rarefied world of desirable grand touring cars. So began a long and quite distinguished lineage of sporting Scimitar models with powerful six-cylinder engines that lasted until the mid 1980s.

Reliant's introduction to the world of design-led products, rather than niche vehicles tightly hemmed in by the strictures of legislation, proved a bit of a sea change. As well as the Scimitar, another arrival in 1964 was the Reliant Rebel, a four-wheeled economy car. It was a remarkably bold grab at a slice of the mainstream economy car market. The mechanical package was familiar from the Regal 3/25, but the new chassis, using an independent front suspension system from the Standard 10, put the engine/gearbox in a conventional position at the front. With its plastic body and 600cc all-alloy motor, the Rebel would be much more economical than its rivals, Mini and Imp included, with 60mph a realistic everyday level, but the higher initial costs were rather off-putting. It was, though, the first whole-car design that Reliant commissioned from their new pal Tom Karen at Ogle, and it was quite a neat little fastback saloon, for which no embarrassed apology needed to be mumbled by those who owned one.

Chugging along profitably all the time, though, was the Regal, but even then the vigorous Mr Wiggin was not idle. For in 1965, he launched the 3/25 Super at £486. In addition to a host of changes to make the interior more inviting (more luxurious would be overstating matters), such as revised trim and a slightly less austere dashboard, Tom Karen at Ogle had been tasked with sprinkling some sophistication over the sharp and angular styling, which was growing old ungracefully. The best he could achieve was a subtle, narrow, twin-aperture air intake in place of the crude drain-cover-style grille of yore, and eradicate some of the jagged, hooded effect over the headlights. Reliant, though, was not an outfit likely to waste anything, so the old-style Regal 3/25 continued alongside, with an £18 price cut.

In 1967, a genuinely upmarket edition of the car joined the range, called the Regal 21E. The tag implied that there were 21 extras thrown in as standard, such as a locking petrol cap, spotlights, chrome on the overriders and door hinges, and not just a spare wheel but a cover to go on it. All for just £64 more, and doubtless carefully costed to bring some extra profit in for Two Gates.

The handsome lines and meaty performance of the Ford V6-powered Scimitar GTE catapulted the previously mundane Reliant name into the world of the beautiful people.

The final major upgrade for the car came along in 1968, when an enlarged 700cc engine was introduced; power was upped to 30bhp and so it was renamed the 3/30.

The cars continued to sell amazingly well, with very little more in the way of modernisation. In 1972, the seventh-generation Regal range hit 100,000 sales (the complete final tally would be 105,824), making it one of the most successful three-wheeled cars of all time. Reliants were an everyday sight across the whole of the UK – a far cry from their stumbling 1953 introduction and tentative arrival as, in effect, a motorbike with a roof and a steering wheel. At the other end of the scale, the Scimitar GTE, with its sporting estate-car bodywork and powerful Ford V6 engine, was being bought and driven by society's beautiful people, led by Princess Anne, who received one as a combined twentieth birthday/Christmas present in 1970 and became a devoted, lead-footed Scimitar driver. But the most famous Reliant of all was still to come.

Four

Bugs and Gutters

The Reliant Robin was revealed to the world in October 1973, after the company had invested £1.75m to create the car and prepare its three plants to make it. Most people couldn't help but agree that it was a radical departure from the dated yet still popular Regal 3/25. But the company had, in fact, already had a go at blowing away the dust from the British three-wheeler, and the experience was a salutary one in terms of how far the boundaries of the genre could be pushed.

As far back as 1955 – and long before he came into the Reliant orbit – Ogle's Tom Karen had nursed a pet project to create a three-wheeled fun car for young people. A nifty runabout with two seats that would be super cheap to run and yet, in a twisted way, also a way to get you noticed by the opposite sex – a bit like the VW-based beach buggies that suddenly became a part of Californian surf culture. He'd done drawings and built models in the past, and once his working relationship with Ray Wiggin was firmly established with the Scimitar and Rebel rolling out of the factory, his timing was perfect to pitch the car as a real-life project. Even Karen was surprised when, after just a few weeks of contemplation, Reliant gave the idea the thumbs-up.

The basic concept was a wedge-shaped two-seater where almost every feature was a clever compromise between trendy design and cheap manufacture. Rather than bother about doors, the cockpit was accessed through a lift-up canopy with a flat windscreen and plastic side screens, and the basic seat shapes were moulded into the glass-fibre base of the body. As there was no rear overhang, a racy feature was made of the exposed back axle, and above that the drop-down lid to the tiny luggage compartment was formed from black-painted plywood. Taking a leaf out of Henry Ford's book, a single colour would reduce manufacturing complexity but, rather than black, a vivid orange was chosen; in tune with product and interiors design influences of the times, for sure, but it would also act as a superb background to the bold, black, racing-car-style body graphics.

The 700cc Reliant engine and gearbox was a direct lift from the Regal, detuned to take account of the car's feather-light weight, but it was mounted on a brand-new chassis. This was the work of highly respected ex-Cooper and Lotus racing-car engineer John Crosthwaite, whom Reliant had recruited to finesse the handling of the Scimitar GT and GTE, and was yet another departure from the make-do-and-mend ethos in which Reliant had evolved. Actually, it was a thoroughly revised rendition of the Regal rolling frame, where elegant design simplifications freed some weight, which Crosthwaite was then able to add back in the form of stronger, heavier gauge steel.

As this intriguing little vehicle was nearing the end of its development process, Reliant pulled off yet another audacious move. In February 1969 it bought its only significant rival in Britain's arcane three-wheeler world, Bond Cars of Preston in Lancashire. With alluring, glamorous overtones of Ian Fleming's 007, the Bond brand was just perfect to give the new car an extra image fillip. And thanks to its cheeky, sprouting

There was only one serious challenge to the three-wheeled supremacy of the Regal in the 1960s: the Bond 875, with a four-cylinder Hillman Imp engine in the tail of its plastic body.

Reliant introduced the Bond Bug in 1970 to an open-mouthed motoring world; nothing else quite like it had been seen before – nor since.

The cover of the 1970 Bond Bug brochure, showing the racy black body graphics and the part it could play in your romantic life.

How cool is that? A dashing young architect (probably) opening up the Bond Bug's plastic canopy; check out the black-painted plywood boot lid, where those rolled-up plans are no doubt going to be stowed.

The Bond Bug must qualify as one of the bravest attempts to inject fun and style into budget motoring for young people; sadly, it was a commercial failure for Reliant.

oblong headlights and chisel-fronted profile, the model name of Bug pretty much suggested itself.

It didn't matter that Reliant had limited resources to devote to the Bug's launch: the car got column attention and public attention in spades, popping up on TV and in advertising promotions. Reliant developed special buying packages, combining hire-purchase terms, insurance and servicing so that it appealed to people in their early 20s. The company even stuck it to the mainstream car industry at the 1970 London Motor Show; three-wheelers were banned, so Reliant built a four-wheeled Bug show car, essentially two Bugs attached back to back.

You really couldn't want for more lateral and imaginative thinking in a single vehicle design. And yet, in the final reckoning, the Bond Bug was a commercial failure. A dismal 2,270 were built in four years. It wasn't just that the car was too outlandish for most tastes, or that early production problems – leading quickly to the closure of Bond's Preston

The Letchworth Hertfordshire headquarters of Ogle Design, the studio which created the Reliant Robin, with the one-off Ogle Scimitar GTE show car in the foreground.

factory and Bug assembly decamping to Tamworth – strangled supply. The economics just didn't stack up. There were three models in a price range from £548 to £628, but they were all sold at a loss, and the most expensive 700ES was undercut by both the Hillman Imp and the Mini. Of course, the Bond Bug just oozed fun, but then again there were only two seats, minimal luggage space, and when all was said and done, it was still a three-wheeler. Even with every bit of imaginative thought they'd thrown at the Bug, perceptions about trikes probably hadn't been shifted much. It was an incredibly brave product – and Bond Bugs really are collectable today – but for Reliant it was a blind alley, and a relatively small, independent company like this one could ill-afford to make mistakes. Now it had devoured its Bond rival, Reliant had the three-wheeler market almost to itself. Making it pay was, from now on, going to be a make or break business.

The failure of the Bug might have engendered a profound sadness in any progressive designer, but Tom Karen, used to working in such tough retail sectors as domestic white goods, was not only pragmatic but was already focused on his wide spectrum of new projects. One of his most important was the next generation of Reliant's core four-seater three-wheelers, and that could only benefit from lessons learnt from the Bug venture.

At the age of 89, Tom Karen revealed to me that he had had a radical rethink of the basic Regal very early on in his dealings with the Tamworth company:

> I was desperate to change it because it wasn't exactly attractive. I really thought their Regal needed improvement, and so in 1963/4 I did a design and made a 1:8 scale model of it. I did the original design on spec. I often wasted my time doing that sort of thing because I was always trying to nudge people into better design.
>
> I think my little model may have softened Ray Wiggin and the management at Reliant up in the long term. John Crosthwaite had joined Reliant, a very good suspension person, who'd worked on the design of Formula 2 cars, and he was anxious to do a new chassis. At some point around then, which must have been 1966 or '67, they decided to update the Regal, and they gave my model approval. The final product was not very different.

A rare surviving picture of the model, which quickly gained the code-name TW8 (Three-Wheeler No. 8, although the numbering system

A very rare image of Tom Karen's model of TW8, completed in 1963–64. It was done on-spec for Reliant because he intensely disliked the dated looks of the Regal 3/25.

must also have delighted old Tom Williams himself), indeed shows remarkable similarity to the Regal's replacement in its overall profile, the reduction in wheel size and the fastback rear end. Tom Karen explained his rationale behind the styling to a writer in *The Guardian* newspaper in January 2014:

> The car's distinctive shape arose from not wanting a boot sticking out at the back, which had made the car version of the Regal look like three boxes stuck together. In 1968, I designed the Scimitar GTE, giving it a gently sloping rear window, which we now call a hatchback, and I kept the look for the Robin.

Tom added, to me, that his hatchback-type rear window was a cost-saving idea in the best Reliant tradition of penny-pinching:

> The glass hatchback was my idea. It was a neat design and, because it used flat glass, it was very inexpensive to make. With Reliant, everything had to come out of a bin, or else be the cheapest item they could get

hold of, but that was part of the challenge. You couldn't design new headlights – they had to be ones that Lucas, or whoever, made already! It's a very neat body as a hatchback and, anyway, I'd always liked little, inexpensive cars.

As to the frontal design, Tom was limited by the technical layout of the car:

There was no point in being dishonest, in design terms, about the fact that it was a three-wheeler. You could narrow the front a little bit to make it not look so boxy. The biggest challenge was coming up with a three-wheeled car that qualified as a motorcycle, meaning it could be driven without a full licence. Even though it's a four-seater with a four-cylinder engine, it still had to weigh less than 8cwt. And this required a lot of innovation.

There is one key thing, though, that Tom found uncommonly pleasing as a progressive design feature. It was on the design model and then present on the finished car, but very few people would notice it if it wasn't pointed out first, despite the fact that it is pertinent to just about every modern car:

I am quite proud of that car, but the thing I'm most proud about is that I got rid of the roof gutters – the drip rail running along the edges of the roof above the doors. It isn't needed. On a steel car, it's there because it's a convenient place to spot-weld the body sections. But on a glass-fibre car, getting rid of it actually saved moulding work.

I hid the gutter inside the roof behind the edge of the door. Actually, I originally wanted the shutline of the door to go right up to the windscreen frame, but Reliant didn't want to do that, so that's why there was a conventional door pillar. It was the first car to do without a drip

rail. Giugiaro did one ten years later for Fiat, which people said was the first, but it wasn't. The Robin was, even though it wasn't a four-wheeler.

By 1971–72, the TW8 had gained its model title of Robin, continuing the policy of choosing cute names of creatures. It was yet another breath of fresh air, banishing the old Regal name, which somehow conjured up pictures of Queen Victoria on the lav or a depressingly stale backstreet cinema showing one of those 'saucy' British sex romps. Meanwhile, Tom and his team at Ogle looked after all the interior design of the Robin. He makes the interesting observation – by today's yardsticks of computer-modelling and 3D printing – that once the final full-size clay models were signed off with Ray Wiggin's management team, they were actually used as the masters from which the glass-fibre moulds were taken.

While so much attention was given to the Robin's body, there was plenty going on in the chassis and powertrain department. John Crosthwaite's Bond Bug chassis formed the basis for the Robin's, extended at the back for the four-seater body, its track narrowed by 2.5in and its wheelbase shortened by an inch. The engine capacity, meanwhile, was increased to 750cc (this version was first seen in the slow-selling Rebel in October 1972) to give some extra vigour to the car's performance. The gearbox now had synchromesh on all four gears. To get the best road manners possible from the three-wheeled layout, a new anti-roll bar was intended to give much-improved cornering, and wheel size reduction to 10in, like the Mini, from the Regal's 12in size made for a suppler ride quality and cut rolling resistance. They were all very worthwhile improvements from Crosthwaite, who had designed racing cars for the Indianapolis 500 in the USA (he died in 2010). However, as Tom recalled, 'The chassis was a given. So were the parts. Nothing about it was an unknown. In fact, it used the Bond Bug chassis which had been proven before the Robin came along.'

Five

Robins and Road Tests

Tom Williams was probably used to launching his new cars with a beer and a ham sandwich in a Tamworth local. Ray Wiggin had other ideas. He hired the Goodwood racetrack in West Sussex and invited 100 journalists and TV reporters, with models on hand to drape themselves over the Robins' bonnets. He also brought along a car artfully cut in half lengthways so the special guests could see at first hand the Robin's inner workings and sound engineering.

Wiggin demonstrated he had learnt the Bond Bug lesson. The new car was aimed primarily at the Reliant faithful. 'Our strategy is a simple one,' he was quoted at the time of the big launch. 'To continue to sell to our traditional ex-motorcycle market while introducing more newcomers each year to the pleasures and economies of three-wheel motoring.'

Immediately after the Goodwood bash – at which, apparently, not one of the cars was overturned by arrogantly gung-ho members of the mainstream car media – the flotilla of launch Robins was dispersed to Reliant dealers around the country. Many of the dealers already knew about the Robin from a launch at Stoneleigh, hosted by the BBC's *Tomorrow's World* anchorman, Raymond Baxter, taking the silver dollar in exchange for his TV kudos. Now it was the dealers' turn to hold their own launch parties.

All things considered, not least of which was the tiny size of Reliant compared to the major carmakers like Ford, British Leyland and Vauxhall, the Robin launch was little short of astounding in its effect.

Sales in 1974, its first year on sale, were exceptionally strong, as they topped 10,000. In spring that year some 300 cars were being built each week. In 1975, sales surged to 15,000. 'Our best customer is the person who already owns a Reliant,' Ray Wiggin had said, but there was a new phenomenon at work here: the 'conquest' sale. Dealers up and down the country were reporting that four-wheeled cars were increasingly being exchanged against a new Robin. Ford Escorts, Vauxhall Vivas and Minis were the main trade-ins.

True, these were three of the most rust-prone of current British cars, but the true reason for the Robin's amazing spurt in popularity lay in geopolitics. Just as the Suez Crisis had boosted Reliant in the 1950s, now the Arab-Israeli war in the Middle East, with its squeeze on petrol supplies and consequent leaps in fuel prices, was making a new Reliant look to being your best bet for truly economical, everyday motoring. Weekly car magazine *Autocar* summed the situation up succinctly in November 1973: 'All told, the Robin marks a real step forward in three-wheeler design. There is no doubt that the £10 a year tax instead of £25 is a powerful incentive to own one. Many people are also attracted by the running costs – at least 45mpg.'

This was even more incredible, though, when you looked at the Robin versus its closest economy car rivals. With a Robin costing £801, it was at least £100 more expensive than a Mini, a Daf 44 or a Fiat 126, so it was seemingly quite uncompetitive. However, those three metal-bodied rivals, all being heavier, were at least 20 per cent less

A photo of a very early Robin 750 showing the alloy-wheel twin-set that was an option for the back. (Ogle Noor Ltd)

Rear view of an early Robin clearly shows the fuel filler, whose low-mounted position led to petrol slopping out. Let's hope that door was ajar rather than so ill fitting. (Ogle Noor Ltd)

This example of the Robin was artfully sliced in half for the press launch at the Goodwood circuit to reveal the car's inner secrets. Seems to be some wasted space above the front wheel.

Left: At the time of its launch, the Robin was deservedly regarded as one of the best-designed three-wheeler economy cars ever. Note the moulded-in bumpers to cut down on the weight of separate metal items.

Right: Paris is a long way from Tamworth, but this very early car made it there, headlights appropriately adjusted, to have its touristy picture taken beneath the Eiffel Tower.

because their frames were as small as possible to save weight. The back seat did fold down so that up to 30 cu.ft of cargo could be stuffed in, but the opening rear window wasn't really a hatchback in the way the tailgate on a Renault 5 was. Finally, Reliant liked to say that the simplicity of its three-wheelers meant that owners could save even more petty cash by doing their own home maintenance, but the engine was a nightmare to access. The removable panels inside the cabin were now deemed too dangerous and had been sealed up, and opening the tiny hatch cover that doubled as a bonnet lid revealed the heater and battery, but everything else was buried deep and unreachable in the bowels of the chassis frame.

There were two Robin saloons to choose from in 1974: the Standard and the Super. They were fundamentally the same things but the semantics of the pecking order resulted in the Super being loaded with extras that, today, seem trivial but, back then, pointed to what an austere offering the Standard Robin really was. The Special's added bonuses included foglamps, overriders, a passenger sun visor, full-diameter hubcaps, a coachline, hazard warning lights, mudflaps and a few splashes of chrome on instruments and grille. It should be said, mind, that over 60 per cent of buyers opted for the Super, which must surely have provided welcome extra profit for Reliant.

Right from the start there were also two Robin vans, the Standard and Super trim levels corresponding to the saloons. With a boxy rear end and a single opening door hinged on the right, this pint-size loadlugger would cope with 5cwt of goods and 40 cu.ft of volume (or 50 cu.ft if the passenger seat was removed). The Standard van cost £764, this Super van £837.

What was the Reliant Robin really like to drive? There can be little doubt that anyone used to twirling a Mini round the roads of Britain could not possibly have felt at home. While a Mini could hold on to the road in the very tightest of corners taken swiftly, the Robin needed care and smoothness. Perhaps fortunately for Reliant, the motoring press rather avoided deep, critical analysis of the early examples, sticking very much to the letter of the law by categorising them as motorbike-related rather than proper cars, so most detailed reports were published in the motorcycling press.

One early such test was of a Robin Super van in the May 1974 issue of *Motorcycle Mechanics*, where the editor Chas Deane drove one for 600 miles. He was warm in his reception for it, praising its 70mph top speed, potential for 60mpg, 'a really good degree of comfort for the

mean with petrol than the three-wheeled rapscallion from the Black Country. And yet, at 22 seconds, the Robin could beat them all to 60mph; only the 73mph Daf was faster than the 72mph Robin.

It was absolutely true, albeit a shock: the Robin, more or less, made sense as a proper alternative to a real car. Well, sort of. Allowances had to be made, you understand.

Ogle Design had made a concerted effort at trying to mask the huge bulge of the car's gearbox, plonked as it was between the driver and front-seat passenger, but there was no avoiding the horribly cramped footwell and minimum amount of shuffle space between the pedals. Then there were the seats, looking like they were designed for gnomes

Robin

A new idea from the ground up

Cover of the very first brochure for the new Reliant Robin in early 1974. You might have thought they could find a better photographic location than this concrete-heavy council estate.

The Robin van was part of the line-up from the very start; this is the Super edition with fog lights, chrome hubcaps and contrasting coachline.

With a payload of 5cwt, and a fairly versatile interior that could make use of the space by removing the passenger seat, this Robin Super van is busy earning its keep.

Above: In order to ward off parking knocks on the 'fake' glass-fibre bumpers, overriders could be fitted, and were indeed standard on the Robin Super. (Ogle Noor Ltd)

Left: This busy press advert for two dealers on the outskirts of London is a fascinating window into the contemporary Reliant world as emphasis shifted from wacky Bond Bug to practical Robin.

average size person' from the diddy seats and the reassuring brakes. He wrote:

> Roadholding, which is far superior to the old Reliant, is reasonable and although the Robin, because of its light weight and hard suspension, seems a little unstable when you first take the controls, it is amazing how far the new three-wheeler can be pushed before it will pick up a wheel at the rear.

Amusingly, Mr Deane devoted some of his report to ways you could improve the vehicle. He extolled the virtues of Reliant's dealer-supplied kit to add two rear seats to the van for just £14.85 and also a set of adhesive felt pads, offered by a company called Two Strokes Ltd, that could be stuck in strategic spots like on the underside of the bonnet, inside the engine compartment and on the floor to cut out the Robin Super van's tiresome mechanical boom when on the move. That was probably the best £9.50 any owner could spend; one wonders how far he got on his 600-mile odyssey before buying a set.

A lack of refinement, though, was not the most serious flaw on the early Robin. Customers found that the poor restraint mechanism meant the doors could crack if you let go of them in a strong wind, but this was soon remedied.

Its Achilles' heel was a petrol tank whose filler pipe was positioned too low on the bodyside. With a full tank whilst on corners taken at anything other than very sedate speeds, petrol was likely to gush back up the filler pipe and spew out through the cap.

This particular fault was fixed in late 1975 after many complaints, at about the same time as the little alloy engine was bored out, yet again, to give an increased capacity of 848cc. Known as the Robin 850, it had a new SU carburettor replacing the old Zenith item and 40bhp instead of its former 32bhp, a rather startling near-25 per cent power increase that slashed a whole 5 seconds from its 0–60mph figure and sent the top speed up to a somewhat hair-raising 85mph.

With this newly enlarged engine, and its fuel tank no longer spilling petrol in S-bends, the Reliant Robin had reached maturity. As they were now an increasingly common sight on British roads, the car media could disdain them no longer. In April 1976, *Autocar* magazine held its nose and subjected a Robin 850 to its road-test treatment. As tested, it cost £1,454, with extras including a £46 radio, a £17 heated rear window and a £22 pair of cast alloy wheels. The reporter was aghast at the high price considering you could get a Mini 850 for less.

The Tamworth manufacturer could have expected sympathy from the bike press, but *Autocar* cast its objective eye over the Robin as if it was any small car. It did not make for happy reading. 'Our test team unanimously concluded that the Robin's handling fails to approach the standards of all but one or two current four-wheel cars,' it opined:

We had the feeling that the 850 was better than the 750 in this respect – there was less of a sensation that you simply *dare* not move the steering wheel from the straight-ahead position at maximum speed – but even so, stability was poor, and the cornering limit is usually set by the tendency of the vehicle to overturn, a rare thing these days in four-wheelers. On poorer surfaces, the single front wheel can sometimes catch out the

Small families on tight budgets could get great value from a Robin, saving enough money to give Asda, Fine Fare and Safeway a wide berth and head for upmarket grocers' shops in the Cotswolds.

A rather charming publicity picture of a Robin Super taken in 1975, with a happy-looking mum and two children, who have been temporarily distracted from whining. Bless.

Tom Karen of Ogle Design had sought to create a 'two-box' (one box for the engine, another for the passengers) fastback look for the Robin to maximise interior space and design harmony.

The new lightweight van that will take a lot of beating

Robin

Very early brochure for the Robin van with the standard-bearer on the cover, resplendent in the sort of lurid yellow that the world adored in the mid 1970s.

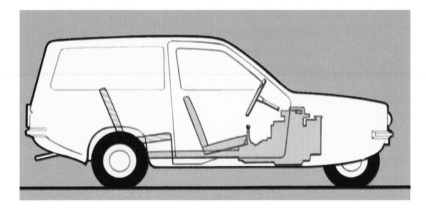

Graphic from the Robin van brochure showing how passenger seats could be installed in the back; as rear-seat passengers sat atop the rear axle rather than within the wheelbase, ride comfort was always on the bumpy side.

driver by developing massive understeer, causing the vehicle to swing very wide of the intended line …

The ride is a long way below modern four-wheel standards, harsh and bumpy, the short wheelbase causing plenty of pitching. The three-wheel layout carries a penalty of its own, in that it is rarely possible, as in a four-wheeler, to run astride a big pothole or lump.

Okay, so they had made their point about three wheels. Their conclusions were largely irrelevant because the vast majority of owners built their style of driving around the Robin's limited capabilities. They tended to be driven slowly and carefully, never hurled into corners or gunned down unsurfaced roads, and few people would have chosen one for a life of relentlessly long journeys on motorways and fast

More smiles per gallon

Up to 60 m.p.g. on 2-star petrol – and there's plenty more to smile about.

Like £10 a year road tax, and a glass fibre body which cannot rust and is its own garage.

How about luggage space? 8½ cubic feet opening up to an incredible 30 cubic feet with the back seat down.

As for performance, that'll make you really happy; 50-60 cruising, 70+ top speed, nimble in traffic and a joy to park.

Perk yourself up – test drive a Robin, the smile-a-mile car.

To: Marketing Services, Reliant Motor Company Ltd., Tamworth, Staffs, B77 1HN
Please send me details of : Robin Saloons from £1076·40 ☐
Robin Vans from £941·22 ☐
Tick here if you would like a test drive arranged for you ☐
Name
Address
Age if under 18
Prices are ex-works and include VAT and car tax.

Robin Makes even Scrooge smile.

Left: Money saving had never been so relevant as in the inflation-spiralling, fuel-scarce 1970s – an economic malaise that Reliant was able to exploit in its Robin advertising.

Below: The new Robin 850, its chocolate-brown paintwork a badge of 1970s honour and its bigger engine now 25 per cent more powerful than before.

A page from the Robin brochure proudly showing the lifting glass hatchback and the folding rear seat that made the car a real picnic to have around.

Robin
a new idea about space

The Robin's rear-window is more than an aid to visibility. It is also a door, the hinges are at the top.

This is how you get into the boot. There are 8½ cubic feet of it – and you load in shopping or luggage 'just like that'.

This is Robin as a saloon. But Robin is a *saloon-estate:* release two catches and the whole back seat folds forward, so you have THIRTY CUBIC FEET of luggage-space – every inch of it easy to see and easy to reach, from inside or outside the car.

Besides which you have a glove-box, and two door-pockets; and, when the back seat is up, a tonneau cover behind it – which, incidentally, protects the contents of the boot from prying eyes.

A roads. With a Robin, the magic statistic was always the 70mpg fuel consumption in store if you could maintain a constant 40mph, and even the most thickheaded driver realised that that could only be achieved with gentle use.

Funnily enough, the 850cc engine liked to be revved but, as *Autocar* discovered, the racket produced in trying to hit 6,000rpm was unbearably deafening: 'The Robin is neither smooth nor quiet except when cruised very gently; 60mph in the Robin reminds you in no uncertain terms that the engine is almost in the cabin with you.'

There were other legitimate moans, including the appallingly inaccessible engine and the unexpectedly large turning circle, but the seats, heating, 30 cu.ft of luggage space, general liveliness and, of course, economy all won praise. *Autocar* concluded by questioning one of Reliant's age-old, money-saving maxims: 'It's some kind of half-way house between a motorcycle and a proper motor car. But that is a strange logic for us. Does the annual tax really loom so large in so many eyes?'

This organ's verdict, of course, reflected its own outlook on motoring. It's illuminating to consider another approach, in January 1976, from

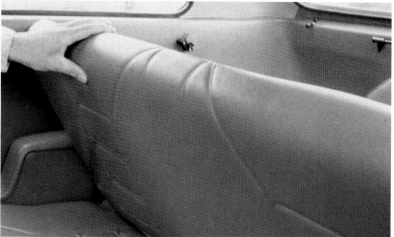

A cocoon of light-brown vinyl characterises the Robin 850 interior in this brochure image. Reassuring to see those sturdily fitted seatbelts.

Another brochure image shows the apparent ease with which the rear seatback could be dropped to increase cargo capacity in the Robin saloon.

The design of a plastic dashboard and console to cover the intrusive engine hump, pictured in a brochure, would survive in successive Robins and Rialtos for some twenty-five years.

lorry and van magazine *Commercial Motor*. It took a Robin 850 Super van on its usual 'light van test route' and, at an average speed of 27mph, was fulsome in its praise for the vehicle's tiny appetite for fuel – the aspect that any business would naturally be concerned with. It achieved 47.2mpg half laden and 34.8mpg with max cargo. The reporter pointed out that while routine services were needed every 6,000 miles, Reliant recommended an interim one after 3,000 miles if the van was being used for lots of stop/start deliveries. Like most other independent critics, it was compelled to point out that engine access was anything but easy if the distributor was playing up or a new oil filter needed fitting.

There was praise for the van's braking and peppy performance in the cut and thrust of urban traffic, as well as the 'lavish' trim of brushed nylon seats and footwell carpeting. Less pleasing were the facts that the load area door was apt to slam shut in the wind and that a heated rear window wasn't supplied as standard. But there was no avoiding the driving experience. Fleet managers poring over *Commercial Motor*

AUTOCAR, w/e 17 April 1976

TEST EXTRA

Reliant Robin 850

Reliant's "three-wheel Kitten" sacrifices a good deal without much obvious gain.
Handling, ride, noise all much worse than average
Performance quite good, economy good but not exceptional
Price high for what it offers.

THERE IS in England this phenomenon known as the three-wheeled brigade, its needs catered for exclusively by the Reliant Motor Company, formerly with the Regal and now with the Robin. When the Robin first emerged *Autocar* took note of the fact but could not bring itself to carry out a proper Road Test; there was still a tacit agreement that three-wheelers were more properly the province of our sister motor-cycling magazines. Since then, however, the Robin acquired first a sister ship in the form of the four-wheeled Kitten, and then itself received the Kitten's

bigger engine and higher gearing. Both these things brought it closer to our sphere of influence, and we decided it was well worth looking at the Robin 850 to see how it compared with current four-wheel standards in general, and with the Kitten (which we mostly liked) in particular.

First, it must be said that three-wheel motoring is not cheap. The Super Robin 850, as tested, lists at £1,454 which is more than the basic Mini 850; but there is a less well equipped Robin which manages to undercut the Leyland car at £1,322. At this price, the seat belts are

Below: Four wheels on my three-wheeler wagon. The Reliant Robin 850 is seen at MIRA on its way to a maximum speed of 77 mph. The bluff front and narrow front/wide rear body shape is evident

Autocar magazine's 1976 road test: the main picture shows the car at speed on the MIRA test track, fitted with what's usually called a 'fifth wheel' – but in this exceptional case a 'fourth wheel' – which helps collect accurate speed and acceleration data.

A footie-mad owner taking delivery of his gleaming new Robin 850 estate from a dealer in around 1976.

Great cover of the early Robin 850 brochure, hinting at what a boon the little car could be for a happy family life.

Haynes sold a large number of their workshop manuals for the Robin (and four-wheeled Kitten) to owners keen to do their own DIY maintenance. It was a very useful book, especially as the Robin's engine was so ludicrously inaccessible. (Haynes Publishing)

in 1976 must have questioned the wisdom of putting members of staff into a Robin van. 'The Robin was delivered for test with a 250kg (550lb) load of sandbags, pushed well towards the front of the van,' the article read:

In this condition, town driving was quite acceptable – in fact, it almost felt as though the van had four wheels.

Motorway driving was a different story, however. Overtaking high-sided vehicles was a nerve-racking manoeuvre at speeds above 50mph, with the Reliant being blown off course when meeting the cross-wind as it passed the front of the vehicle being overtaken. Great concentration was called for and steering wheel movements were necessary to maintain a straight course. Presumably the unladen state produces even more unnerving situations.

Low-speed steering seemed heavy for such a small, light vehicle – possibly owing to the small steering wheel Reliant fits. This size of wheel

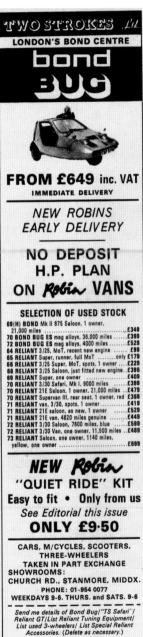

is essential to allow all but the most diminutive of drivers to gain access to the driving seat.

On the ride and handling section at MIRA's [the Motor Industry Research Association at Nuneaton, Warwickshire] proving ground, the Robin behaved fairly well, although a few uneasy moments were experienced when negotiating the adverse camber portion of the circuit.

Nonetheless, the summary was positive: 'For the operator who needs an economical, lightweight, 254kg (5cwt) capacity delivery van, the Super Robin would seem to offer many advantages, at a basic price of £1,301.94. The price of the Robin as tested was £1,443,26.'

In 2015, a similar Robin van made an appearance alongside Dame Maggie Smith in Alan Bennett's movie *The Lady In The Van*, although it should be pointed out that Miss Shepherd spent her nights not folded up in the back of this one, but in a Bedford CA and a Commer.

Above: Reliant, along with other European carmakers, faced extra competition in the British new-car market, with the 1974 launch of Russia's Lada, which carried artificially low prices for a full-size, four-wheeled saloon.

Right: Advertising from London dealer Two Strokes trying to clear unsold Bond Bugs, drum up Robin business, and interest owners in spending a tenner to enjoy reduced racket inside the little cars.

Six

Successes and Scandals

We now find ourselves in 1977, the year of punk, the first/fourth *Star Wars* movie, take-off for the Space Shuttle and scheduled transatlantic Concorde flights, and the Queen's Silver Jubilee; indeed, Reliant issued a limited edition of 750, individually numbered Jubilee Robins, finished in Royal purple with silver highlights, and they sold like hot cakes. The manufacturer had also quietly added a Robin estate to its line-up, essentially a van with rear side windows and folding bench seat.

Reliant really was a remarkable enterprise. In 1960, annual turnover stood at £700,000, shooting up to £3m when the energetic Ray Wiggin took the company helm in 1964, and now, in 1977, it was £21m. It had produced 176,000 of its own light alloy engines. With the Robin as its staple product, the range also included the four-wheeled Kitten (replacing the Rebel in 1975) and the second-generation Scimitar GTE. Its yearly output of 12,000 vehicles made it, after the ailing conglomerate of British Leyland, the second-largest British-owned car manufacturer. The firm's budget engineering experience had seen it set up low-cost vehicle manufacturing plants in Israel, Greece and Turkey.

Reliant was the biggest carmaker in Europe that used glass fibre for its bodies, and they were all produced at the company's 106,000 sq.ft plant at Kettlebrook. In 1977 some 430 people toiled there, able to turn out 20,000 complete bodies a year, and while there were hot-press mouldings for doors and bonnets made on matching dies, most of the work – building up layers of glass fibre and resin – was done by hand.

The company liked to tell visitors that the strands of glass fibre it used were only 0.0003in in diameter yet possessed a tensile strength of up to 400,000lb per square inch, which, it said, was a higher strength/weight ratio than the finest quality steels. Nonetheless, as Reliant staff set about cutting sixty layers at a time from newly delivered rolls of glass-fibre mat, using razor-sharp steel-alloy knives, it can't have looked too promising as a material for a car body.

Each Robin body consisted of about 160 mat pattern pieces. Resin with a catalyst was added, followed by 'laying up' the glass-fibre sheets while working resin thoroughly into them. This was called 'wetting out', and mouldings would be revolved through 360 degrees so that the sides, roof and floor could be built up conveniently.

Mouldings were washed, dried, polished, gel-coated with a polyester resin and cured between each process and, with three ovens on the go, a moulding was ready every six minutes. Mouldings then moved to trim shops where excess material was cut away, edges sanded to a smooth finish and holes drilled for later insertion of electrical and other fittings. And it comes as no surprise to learn that each part was weighed to make sure the little car's strict adherence to legal limits was met.

After thorough cleansing, outer bodies were heated in an oven to reveal any air bubbles, imperfections were rectified with filler, and the doors and bonnets were attached to the bodies. The finely finished inner and outer sections of the Robin shell would move along a tracked

Left: A satisfyingly colour-coordinated brochure group shot of the unlikely Reliant line-up in 1977: Robin to the left, Kitten to the right and the luxury Scimitar GTE in the background.

Above: In 1975 the strong-selling Scimitar GTE was completely revised as the SE6 model, retaining the much-admired, familiar profile but being longer, wider, roomier and more powerful.

Left: Fascinating view of the Robin production line at Tamworth in 1973, with vans and saloons easing their way up and along the twin assembly tracks. (Elvis Payne)

Reliant decided to have another pop at the four-wheeled economy car sector with its 1975 Kitten, adapted from the Robin but with the engine brought forward and a Triumph Herald front-suspension system fitted.

Styling for the Kitten came, as was by now customary, from Ogle Design, the task undertaken by youthful emloyee Peter Stevens, later to design the 213mph McLaren F1 supercar.

production line, as they were bonded together before setting off on the 6-mile journey to the main assembly plant at Two Gates.

The Robin's engine hailed from another Reliant facility at Shenstone, 7 miles away. This place took on the engine-building activity in November 1963 when it was opened by the then reigning Formula 1 World Champion Jim Clark. This 93,000 sq.ft plant employed 300 people making the little power units. Actually, over 90 per cent of the engineered mechanical parts for the Robin were made here, which included gearboxes, rear axles and front suspension parts. After quality and test inspections had been completed, the parts were palleted and loaded on to articulated lorries for their trip to Two Gates.

Ah, yes, Two Gates, the former bus garage site where every Reliant three-wheeler car had come together; it remained the company HQ in 1977, employing over 1,000 in chassis fabrications, paint shops,

trim and upholstery, and full final assembly, as well as design, admin, distribution and sales.

Each completed Robin chassis frame was given two coats of protective paint in an automated dipping plant. Meanwhile, Robin bodies from Kettlebrook progressed along rails through a three-stage painting process, and all carpeting, sound-deadening materials and seat upholsteries were cut, sewn and ribbed in the soft-trim department. Final assembly took place on twin conveyor tracks. After a final quality audit of paintwork, trim and finish, each Robin was weighed to confirm it was within the 8cwt limit and then given a 'short but methodical' road test by Reliant personnel.

Things were going well at the company as 1977 dawned and Robin sales remained buoyant. They were certainly helped by the fact that tricycles were not subject to the same hire purchase restrictions that

A Kitten estate was a natural addition to the range, and probably provided the best possible combination of Reliant economy and usefulness.

customer base, and in Austria where Felber & Company of Vienna held the franchise. By 1977, the Kitten and Scimitar were also being built in left-hand drive form, and Reliant was making a concerted push to market its unusual roster of products in mainland Europe. At various times, a small number of Robins were also assembled in far-flung corners worlds away from Tamworth, including in Greece, Israel and Turkey, generally from kits of parts exported from Britain.

Events, though, were about to cast dark clouds over this otherwise optimistic picture.

The first one was very much behind the scenes and concerned the company's ownership. Tom Williams had sold the controlling interest in the business he founded in 1962 to Gwent & West of England Enterprises, owned by financier Julian (later Sir Julian) Hodge. Its expertise in structuring car loans and hire purchase agreements had been of enormous help in expanding Reliant sales, hugely boosting the market for the Regal 3/25 and then the Robin. Only a 20 per cent down payment was needed, with the remainder repayable over three years.

affected four-wheeled cars, which made them available to many people who otherwise couldn't have afforded a new car.

Reliant's most famous patron, Princess Anne, became a Robin owner. One cannot imagine that she paid for the honour, but rather accepted the bright-pink car as a gesture, for which the company's PR agency, Woolf Laing Christie & Partners, must have been well chuffed. 'I delivered Princess Anne's to Buckingham Palace,' recalled Reliant engineer Dave Peek. 'I think it was for the household staff, but she had several Scimitars, and it was good of her to support the company. I remember giving that Robin a service at the Palace, but many owners simply serviced them themselves.'

There were even a few export prospects opening up for these most peculiarly British of conveyances, particularly in Holland where the Waayenberg family of Veenendaal had built up a small but loyal

A 1976 brochure for the Kitten, which looked undeniably cute and got good notices from critics for its low petrol thirst and tidy, predictable road manners.

In 1973, Hodge then sold his businesses to Standard Chartered Bank, and four years later the new owner decided to offload Reliant to a Kettering-based company called J.F. Nash Securities for a reported £287,000, a conglomerate involved in all kinds of businesses, including distributing caravans. The sale cannot have been unrelated to a dramatic 30 per cent fall in Robin sales in the first four months of 1977, but the company blamed inflation for reducing the purchasing power of those on modest incomes. New owner John Nash declared the car company would continue to operate autonomously, but this didn't ring true with Ray Wiggin, who left the firm he had helped expand so cleverly within six months after his future plans were vetoed by the new guv'nor. He was immediately replaced as managing director by the former personnel manager, Ritchie Spencer.

Trouble, however, was brewing on a separate front, and the Robin was directly in the firing line. The car developed a defect far more serious than anything experienced previously. On several early examples, owners found that the bolts securing the steering box could work themselves loose; once it had come adrift, steering control could be lost entirely, with potentially lethal results. The new management of the company, occupied as it was with trying to make Reliant more efficient and profitable, seemed to turn a deaf ear to the issue, as owners made their fears clear to the dealer network. It was a catastrophic error of judgement. Angry customers, unable to get acknowledgement of the problem from Reliant, turned to the media and watchdogs for help, and before very long the Reliant Robin was being lambasted on national television by BBC1's *That's Life* and in print by the Consumers' Association and its magazine *Which?* The issue even cropped up in the comedy routine of Jasper Carrott. Sentiment towards three-wheelers was further poisoned by another, unrelated, national furore about the blue AC Invacar trikes issued by the NHS to disabled drivers and their suspect safety.

The subject of the Robin's steering malady was even discussed in Parliament in May 1979, and Minister of Transport Norman Fowler said he was aware of several component failures and two fatal accidents involving Robins and that he was 'greatly concerned' at reports of other faults in the cars.

A photo taken from the Robin 850 brochure. Whatever independent road testers opined about the car, it invariably gave a good account of itself if driven with care and gentleness.

Hmm, well, this driving situation might have been shown in the brochure but sustained high speed on blustery motorways was where the Robin was least at home, unless you enjoyed white knuckles.

If you can tear your eyes away from the colossally flared trousers of this Bay City Rollers wannabe busy with his Saturday job, then you'll admire the wide opening door and low loading height of the Robin Super van.

All Reliant publicity images show the Super versions of the Robin, rather than the depressingly austere base models; so here is a Super estate about to do what every 1970s dad loved – setting off to the council tip.

The last hurrah for the original Robin after its protracted media roasting was this 1981 GBS special edition, with gleaming white paintwork and fetching tartan upholstery.

The Reliant Fox was a small, four-wheeled utility vehicle, based on the Kitten and designed in Greece. From 1983, a few hundred were sold in the UK, where Tandy Industries introduced this tiny camper van conversion.

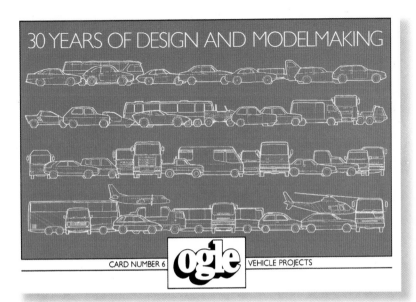

A publicity card issued in 1984 by Ogle Design shows the Robin in its vehicle design chronology – second row down, just right of centre.

Among the most famous of Ogle's vehicle designs were these two Popemobiles for the Pontiff's UK visit in 1982, work undertaken just as the studio's relationship with Reliant was in its dying days.

Whether or not the Robin was fundamentally dangerous, there remained the acrid whiff of scandal and corporate ambivalence. In late 1979, under government pressure, Reliant was forced to issue a grudging recall of 25,000 Robins so that a cradle and strut could be added to shore up the steering-box mounting. The work was done – for free – by Reliant dealers and 47,000 letters were sent out to owners listed on the DVLC register, urging them to pass it on to any new owner, had they sold the car on. In some cases, the 1973–75 cars needed a completely new steering column. The whole sorry episode was one Reliant might have avoided if it had acted more swiftly, but the damage had been done: the Reliant Robin had been shamed, and now it was increasingly shunned.

In 1981, with Robin sales having bombed during a biting recession that should otherwise have seen them booming, John Nash wielded his axe. Two-thirds of the workforce was laid off, the Shenstone factory was shut and engine manufacture transferred to the Two Gates plant and, although the Nash family remained in overall control, the company was listed on the stock market as Reliant Motor PLC in a bid to raise more working capital.

And what of the Robin? There was another limited edition model in mid 1981, the gleaming white GBS, standing for Great British Special and laden with additional comfort and style touches, but as the tumultuous year drew to a close, the last batch of Robins left the production line. An era was over.

'I think the car worked and it had a good following,' Tom Karen told me. 'I'm not at all ashamed of it; I make no apologies at all for it. But it was a declining market. Young people started to get driving licences for cars from the start so they could drive old bangers … which were at least proper cars. Drivers of powerful cars might look down their noses, but the Robin was designed for a particular market. If you're making a car with a price tag of a few hundred pounds, you can't build a Rolls-Royce.'

Seven

Rialto and Revival

Many facets of the 'old' Reliant business – built up as the idiosyncratic vision of the gruff founder Tom Williams and his anointed successor, the rather more urbane Ray Wiggin – altered after the company changed hands in 1977. Some unprofitable products were dropped and the design relationship with Ogle was severed. Most importantly, the philosophy shifted away from trying to increase the skinflint customer base for three-wheelers to chasing buyers with discretionary spend. Such people had lapped up the Scimitar GTE, and now Reliant intended to exploit British Leyland's retreat from small sports cars by designing a two-seater roadster to fill the gap in the market left by the axing of the creaky MG Midget, MGB and Triumph Spitfire. The thinking was sound but the car that emerged in 1984, the Reliant Scimitar SS1, turned out to be a troubled undertaking.

In the meantime, though, and despite the Robin's tarnished image, it would have been folly to throw away the goodwill that persisted among most of the Reliant three-wheeler-owning community.

So, in around 1980, Ritchie Spencer and his cronies contracted a new partner, International Automotive Design (IAD) of Worthing, Sussex, to look at the Robin, and its legislative restrictions, and come up with something that could exorcise its recent demons and propel the motorised trike into the 1980s. IAD, which was founded by Australian engineer John Shute, had only been in business for four years, but there was actually a link to Reliant already in place, in that its director

of design Eddie Pepall had been resident technical artist and designer at Reliant from 1962 until 1965, where he had worked on both the Israeli Sabra and early Scimitar sports cars.

The new broom swept into action on 13 January 1982 when the next generation of Reliant three-wheelers was unveiled. The Robin name had vanished and in its place was Rialto, another title summoning up the image of a fleapit cinema or crummy bingo hall in a dreary, dead-end town, much as Regal had done before 1973.

Immediately obvious was the brand-new front and rear styling. The more wedge-shaped nose had a raked back and black plastic grille bracketed by rectangular headlights (borrowed from the Austin mini-Metro). Replicas of wraparound bumpers were now moulded into the nose and bodysides, with (on the GLS) black plastic bump strips front and rear to ward off slight parking knocks. The back end had suggested bumpers wrapping round the newly squared-up contours from one rear-wheel arch to the other. Longer rear-side windows terminated in what passed for a hatchback-style rear on the saloon. Yet here was one of the shocks of the new car. The clever glass tailgate had been jettisoned for a fixed rear screen with, below it, a drop-down boot lid like a Mini's. True, the loading height had been lowered but it seemed like a major retrograde step. Why Reliant didn't upgrade to a full hatchback in the modern idiom was utterly bewildering. Yet another key feature of the Robin had been changed for the worse too, with ugly rain gutters now tacked on along the windscreen pillars and roof parapets.

Cover of the very first brochure for the new Reliant Rialto range upon its introduction in early 1982.

The opening line-up for the new Rialto featured both saloon and estate variants, along with the van from which the estate was derived.

This angle shows the drop-down boot and the addition of roof gutters, both of which were sacrilege to the original Robin concept from Ogle Design.

As well as much-increased glass area, the new Rialto also had 'suggested' bumper mouldings extended around the corners of the car, which met the wheel arches at the rear.

The prominence of the petrol pump on this flyer for the Rialto stressed the low economy to be savoured, which was quite apposite once more as yet another recession was hobbling Britain in the early 1980s.

This high-gloss image of the new Reliant graced the cover of the firm's 1981 Annual Report, the document that delivered the depressing news of a £1m loss for the previous year.

At the back, the estate and van were much as the old Robin equivalents, albeit with the new, squared-off wheel arches helping to banish memories of the more ovular Robin. In fact, the doors on all models were unchanged from the Robin ones.

A seriously good improvement was the chassis, now fully hot-dip galvanised against corrosion rather than merely painted. The steering had also been made lighter, with a better 27ft turning circle, and suspension height was raised slightly at the front for better ride quality. Another huge benefit was two detachable panels on the engine shroud inside the car, massively improving engine access and, while the dashboard was much like the Robin's, the knobs and switches were more robust, with the windscreen washer and wiper now on a steering column stalk.

And guess what: a heated rear window and a spare wheel were now standard across the board. Hooray. Squeezing in the spare – for so long a near-essential in any road vehicle – within the 8cwt limit must have been quite a victory for the engineers, especially as the Rialto had 10 per cent more glazing area than the old Robin. Here's how they

If the frontage of the Rialto estate seems strangely familiar then that's no surprise; the headlights were hijacked from the Austin mini-Metro, installed either side of a very Metro-like plastic grille.

The ill-fated Scimitar SS1, launched in 1984, on which Reliant invested heavily and pinned its hopes for future prosperity, only to face bitter disappointment.

The Rialto 2 is greeted with a new brochure and renewed focus on economy, with a high-torque edition of the familiar 848cc engine.

RIALTO 2

more style... even MORE economy

did it: they reduced the heavy, metal leaf springs in the rear suspension to just one on each side and gave the windscreen a single wiper. In a Reliant, as at Tesco's, every little helps.

There were five Rialto models: a two-door saloon and three-door estate in plain or fancy GLS trim and a van. Prices ranged from £2,769 to £3,724, the main extras on offer being a £75 push-button radio and £27.50 radial tyres. 'Wherever you look, Rialto is saving you money not wasting it,' was a resonant sentence from the brochure, and that was salient once again in 1982 as the UK crawled agonisingly out of yet another economic recession. A Rialto, driven gently, could return 70mpg, and the owner only had to fork out £28 annual road tax instead of £70 for a proper car.

After the chagrin of the Robin recall, not to mention the slowly dwindling pool of existing customers, the new start was understandably modest. Reliant soon produced forty Rialtos a week, a shadow of the Robin's 330-a-week peak in 1975, but making for solid business nonetheless. Actually, after less than two-and-a-half years, over 7,000 Rialtos had been delivered, an average of about sixty cars weekly. Once again, it might not sound like a hill of beans, but we were well into the era of the excellent modern hatchback like the Austin Metro, Ford Fiesta, Renault 5 and Volkswagen Polo, with the game shortly to be raised by the Fiat Uno and Peugeot 205. Other Rialto alternatives continued to be the evergreen Mini and cheap-and-nasty imports from the Soviet Bloc including FSOs, Ladas and Skodas.

Against all the odds, that funny little three-wheeler from Tamworth was back in the game and in 1984 came the Rialto 2, with a new radiator grille, black-finished bumpers and rain gutters, improved interior trim and, most importantly of all, a so-called 'High Torque-Economy' version of the venerable 850cc Reliant engine. Engine torque was boosted by 7.3 per cent from 46 to 49.5lb ft by a host of small engineering

Among minor design tweaks for the Rialto 2 were black bumpers that gave a degree of deformable protection for the plastic bodywork from head-on or tail-on parking bashes.

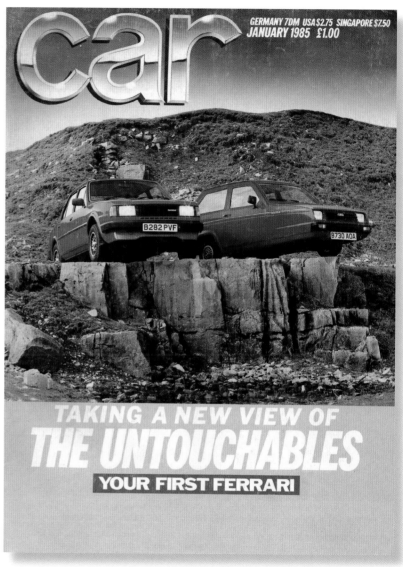

GERMANY 7DM USA $2.75 SINGAPORE $7.50
car JANUARY 1985 £1.00

TAKING A NEW VIEW OF
THE UNTOUCHABLES
YOUR FIRST FERRARI

The Rialto 2 estate was one of the three-wheeler range that helped Rialto sales to hit 10,000 in February 1985 – quite an achievement considering Reliant's somewhat tarnished reputation.

The memorable front cover of *Car* magazine in 1985 when it turned its erudite attention to the Reliant Rialto and other disreputable bargain-basement cars.

Californian company Zoe Industries proposed adapting the Rialto for sale in the USA with a super-wide back axle, although the plan came to nothing; they couldn't even get the spelling of Volkswagen right on this sales leaflet.

changes to camshaft, distributor and carburettor, leading to a 14.7 per cent higher compression ratio from 9.5:1 to 10.5:1. Power output was cut from 40 to 37.5bhp. Still, the lower engine speeds gave even more miserly fuel thirst, with 50mpg easily available in everyday driving and 73mpg at a steady 56mph. Those figures, as Reliant gleefully pointed out, were better than could be had from many motorbikes.

In January 1985, the erudite and entertaining *Car* magazine decided to take a break from testing the latest BMWs and Porsches and reappraise the ultra-budget end of the car market. It led to it publishing one of its most droll cover stories ever, boldly entitled, 'Taking a new view of The Untouchables'. The story looked at the bargain basement merits of the Citroën 2CV, Lada Riva, Skoda Estelle and, of course, the latest Reliant Rialto 2. The three-wheeler was in for a roasting, but Steve Cropley's editorial was at least even-handed: 'Although we could never recommend a Reliant to anyone, even that had a lusty, frugal engine, and quite a well styled dash and interior.'

In the story's introduction, the magazine justified its sampling of the Rialto:

> The Skoda and Reliant chose themselves because they are so universally condemned by reports in organs as disparate as *Motoring*, *Which?* and *Country Life*. Such unanimity among scribblers is suspect. Motoring writers criticise Skodas and Reliants because it is safe to do so – they use the cars to maintain credibility – by showing that they can criticise *something*.

When writing in detail about the Rialto, the magazine noted its positive aspects. It found the gearchange quick and precise, the steering light, and the engine flexible. And 'spectacular' fuel economy. It also found that it could hit 80mph but … 'the problem for that machine is that it's none too stable when the speeds reach the 80s.' No wonder Reliant only quoted a top whack of 75mph. It was the usual story: away from the world of the dedicated and forgiving three-wheeler user, the little car didn't stack up:

> For those who drive to cover distances quickly, the car is dreadfully unstable, both on corners taken quickly and in quite gentle crosswinds. If the wind gets at all fierce, the safest thing to do is to stop. The Rialto is not worth considering for those who have any prospect of passing their four-wheeled licence test.

In 1986, a proper hatchback third rear door was added to the Rialto for the SE model, making the car much more versatile.

For any other vehicle, such verdicts would have sounded a certain death knell. But not for the Rialto. Five weeks after the sobering *Car* piece hit news stands, the 10,000th was built. Despite the miners' strike – which affected a large part of the Reliant customer base – sales held up, and although Reliant was losing money hand over fist, it was because of the multiple, costly disasters experienced with its SS1 sports car.

Three-wheeler development continued. In late 1985, the company reverted to its former 40bhp, non-high torque engine for the very lightly facelifted Rialto SE range (the chief external changes were body-length stripes between front and rear bumper ends, giving the illusion of extra sleekness). A year later and Reliant finally added a proper lift-up tailgate to create the Rialto SE Hatch.

There was also, briefly, the tantalising prospect of the Reliant Rialto being a hit in California. A strange outfit called Zoe Motors Inc. was casting about for small, low-emission vehicles to market around LA

and San Francisco and decided that the Rialto estate had untapped potential as a low-cost (under $6,000) runabout aimed at young drivers. Unconstrained by British road laws, they created a prototype with a vastly wider rear axle, which necessitated hugely flared-out rear wheelarches to accommodate the greatly increased track. It's quite amusing to learn that the great Larry Shinoda, who had been closely involved in the design of several classic Chevrolet Corvettes and Ford Mustangs, was a consultant to the company, and so quite probably had a hand in refashioning Britain's most controversial small car to make it less likely to topple over. Zoe also remodeled the interior, including fitting much more supportive bucket seats than the Rialto's mean little chairs.

The car was unveiled in 1986 and christened the Zoe Z/3000 Series, notionally available in either estate or van form and with lofty talk of offering electric and even petrol-electric hybrid versions suited to California's smog-ridden freeways. The company produced a promotional video (now available for all to see on YouTube), a gem of exceptional 1980s advertising cheese, which even featured an endorsement from the Revd Richard Duncan. The smiling, bearded man of faith claimed to have covered over 150,000 miles on the West Coast in his 750cc Robin over four and a half years.

Alas, the parent firm Zoe Products Inc. – which had once been a distributor of vitamin supplements – became a notorious 'penny share' on Wall Street, amid accusations from the American Securities & Exchange Commission that Zoe's share price-boosting announcements were bogus. By October 1986, the company disappeared, its investors having lost their shirts on their punt as its value fizzled to almost nothing. And the bizarre, Americanised Rialto, or Zoe Z/3000 ST, does not appear ever to have reached customers.

Back to Britain – with a bump. By October 1988, when cumulative Rialto production reached 22,000, the Hatch was accounting for 65 per cent of sales and, at £5,350, it also happened to be the most expensive model in the line-up. But a much bigger surprise followed in 1989. To the delight of marque devotees, the Robin name returned. The new Robin LX replaced the SE Hatch, whose rear body architecture it retained, but it had an all-new frontal treatment, with smoother contours, a low-set air intake and brand-new headlamps and indicators, pirated this time from the Ford Fiesta MkII. Customers loved the old-name/new-look car and orders poured in.

Eight

Wobbling and Welcoming

The Reliant company was about to enter remorselessly choppy corporate waters. In 1990, the Nash family sold its controlling stake to two property developers, who, through a reverse takeover, got their hands on Reliant's stock market listing, but their financial wizardry evaporated when the property market slumped. In October 1990, Reliant was declared bankrupt for the first time ever and official receivers started looking for a new owner for the car-making division.

Just before this happened, I paid the first of several visits to Tamworth to interview key people involved in successive revival

Reliant was plucked from the jaws of oblivion by Beans Industries. One of the subsequent benefits was this new company logo, soon seen on the bonnet of all new cars.

attempts; hence, in September 1990, I found myself interviewing the somewhat cold and defensive Mike Bennett, the firm's marketing director (discovering shortly afterwards that he had plenty to be cheesed-off about).

On the revival of the Robin nomenclature, he was anything but chirpy, saying wearily, 'Robin is a name that we can't escape.' He was, however, pragmatic about the car itself and its buyers:

> It's a declining market rather than an ailing one. The market's changed, though. It used to appeal to young people with a motorcycle driving licence, but now young people are into cars earlier, or stick to flashy scooters instead. But we turn over £5m a year from three-wheelers and if they still make money when we make just 500 a year then we will continue to do that. If they don't, then we'll chop them out.

The eventual buyer of Reliant, in August 1991, was Beans Industries, an engineering company based in Tipton. This firm had been making Reliant engines and other parts under contract since the late 1980s – work that represented a third of its turnover – so it was a major creditor, which probably made it a dejected custodian of the Robin and its ancestry. Nonetheless, the managing director, Lou O'Toole, realised there was demand for a steady thirty cars a week. I was back there in August 1992, shortly after he'd rationalised the Two Gates plant in line with his modest plans for the company.

The useful rear cargo space of the Rialto was far easier to exploit with a proper hatchback; note the lifting parcel shelf to cover the boot area from prying eyes.

Take a fresh look at Reliant

A blunt, plain-speaking man, Mr O'Toole declared Tamworth, 'a bloody awful place to make cars.' He didn't appear to be much of a Robin fan, as he talked about ideas to revive the Scimitar SS1 and tying up a deal with a Russian company for a small, four-wheeled utility vehicle. 'We could then have a similar arrangement for the three-wheeler,' he added, before saying, 'The three-wheeler is our bread-and-butter, while the Sabre and Scimitar is our jam and cream. We believe the future of the company is in four-wheeled cars.'

A minor watershed was reached in October 1992, when the Society of Motor Manufacturers & Traders, for so long hostile to trikes, finally relaxed its rules so that the Robin could be displayed at the British Motor Show at Birmingham's National Exhibition Centre. There, visitors could contemplate the range that now consisted of the Robin LX, the Rialto SE in saloon and estate form, and the Rialto van. Also on proud display for the 1993 year was the Robin LE 93 special edition, temporarily joining its siblings to commemorate forty years of Reliant cars. By September 1993, though, all other models, bar the Robin

The Robin returns! It's 1989 and the most famous sub-brand in three-wheelers is revived with a new model after a hiatus of eight years.

The new Robin LX had a restyled front, but continued Reliant's policy of nicking headlights from other cars, this time the Ford Fiesta MkII.

Under ownership of Beans Industries, the Rialto van was reintroduced to the range, shown here with the Robin and Rialto estate in this brochure image.

DIAMOND ROBIN

RELIANT MOTORS LTD

The Robin Pedigree

The Diamond Robin has a character all of its own. Luxurious and fun to drive, it is also extremely reliable and very cost effective to run.

The steel chassis is built for strength and fully galvanised for a long life. The reinforced glass-fibre body has proven to be tough and highly durable.

The Diamond Robin may be small and unassuming but it's big enough to deliver a top speed in excess of the legal limit and safely carry four persons.

Powered by the latest version of the renowned Reliant 848cc alloy engine. Built in Tamworth, this engine has served customers around the world for decades. Constant quality control and recent improvements ensure that you can expect impressive fuel economy.

The Diamond Robin is equally at home touring the country-side or running around town. It is easily manoeuvred and has plenty of space to carry the shopping.

The Diamond Robin is hand built with pride. Servicing is quick and efficient, spare parts are inexpensive. As rust is not a problem, a regularly serviced engine will ensure the Diamond Robin gives you many years of low cost motoring.

Diamond Robin 60th Anniversary Special Edition

Our top of the range Robin, fully featured, to celebrate 60 years of motor manufacturing an achievement we are very proud of.

Finished in beautiful Pearlescent Diamond White and based on the Robin hatchback. This special edition also offers; luxury grey leather seating, stereo radio/ cassette (with CD socket), rear washer/wiper, stylish front driving lights and heated rear window all as standard.

Photographed at Drayton Manor Park, Tamworth

For one unhappy year, Reliant was owned by the Avonex engineering company, which launched this limited edition Robin to mark Reliant's 60th anniversary in 1995.

RELIANT MOTORS LTD
THE 850 PICK-UP
The Reliant Pedigree
The Reliant 850 has a character all of its own. Rugged and fun to drive, it is extremely reliable and very cost effective to run.
The steel chassis is built for strength and fully galvanised for a long life. The reinforced glass-fibre body has proven to be tough and highly durable.
The 850 Pick-up may be small and unassuming but it's big enough to deliver a top speed in excess of the legal limit and safely carry a pay load of 254kg (5cwt).
Powered by the latest version of the renowned Reliant 848cc alloy engine. Built in Tamworth, this engine has served customers around the world for decades. Constant quality control and recent improvements ensure that you can expect excellent fuel economy.
Ideal for running around town, easily manoeuvred and parked. The 850 Pick-up has plenty of space for carrying.
The 850 Pick-up is hand built with pride. Servicing is quick and efficient, spare parts are inexpensive. As rust is not a problem, a regularly serviced engine will ensure the 850 Pick-up will give you many years of low cost use.
850 Pick-up
This new ¼ tonner pick-up from Reliant incorporates versatility with economy to provide a handsome robust business/pleasure vehicle. The specially designed side opening tailgate allows easy access to the full length of the cargo load area. Optional extras include a protective liner, an external roll bar (ideal for supporting ladders or lengths of timber) and spot lights. The 850 Pick-up costs no more to tax than a motorcycle.
PICK UP
Photographed at Drayton Manor Park, Tamworth

The 850 pickup was created by the Avonex management, but the firm was back in receivership before it could reach showrooms.

LX hatchback, had been dropped, the remaining car gaining minor improvements to heater, brakes and dashboard.

Yet in November 1994, Beans itself was in receivership, pulling Reliant and Lou O'Toole's masterplan down with it. A Tewkesbury engineering firm called Avonex acquired Reliant but fared no better, and the company was in receivership yet again inside a year. It looked as if the most idiosyncratic British motor vehicle of all simply couldn't cheat death this time.

At about this time, in my seemingly endless string of journalistic assignments into the Reliant world, the BBC's *Top Gear* magazine sent me to find out about Michaels of Selby, the Yorkshire-based dealer that, for many years, had sold about 20 per cent of Reliant's three-wheeled output. It clinched the agency in November 1974, just one month after the launch of the original Robin. The company's homespun commercials on Yorkshire TV during the 1970s were rarely off the air and were a small, weird part of the soundtrack of my childhood.

Now I met John Powell, owner of the world's biggest Reliant dealer, situated a few miles south of York, as Reliant's future teetered on the brink of extinction. Even in 1996, they sold ninety new cars and 300 second-hand ones annually. John painted a marvellously precise picture of the real marque stalwarts who'd kept demand alive for so very long. 'They're not image-conscious people; they're basic, honest and very loyal – they're, you know, nice people,' he explained:

> When we started, Reliant customers were treated like second-class citizens. We set out to treat them properly. The traditional customer is from the East or West Riding, places like Leeds, Bradford, Rotherham, Mexborough, Wakefield.
>
> He's probably been, or still is, a miner, a mill worker, perhaps a steel worker. He started with a motorbike for getting to work, then had a motorbike-and-sidecar, and moved to a Reliant because he can drive it on a bike licence – and because it's very cheap to run. I enjoy speaking to my customers. I try to think of myself as a friend of anyone who comes into the showroom. People trust us.
>
> Frankly, the quality of them isn't brilliant but people like them and we have to please the Reliant man – he's our bread and butter.

Just about the only thing that wasn't welcome was a four-wheeled car as a part-exchange against a new Reliant. 'Er, well, we can't really sell them, you see, because that's not what our customers want.'

Nine

Determination and Demise

Against all the odds, in March 1996, a new consortium of investors had decided to give Reliant another try. Indian engineering company San Motors, a businessman called Kevin Leech from the Channel Islands and ex-Jaguar engineer Jonathan Heynes joined forces to stump up £450,000 for the buy-out.

I was soon back in Tamworth to meet Heynes and have another tour of the plant. The Two Gates site was looking more rundown than ever, but Heynes was upbeat. His father, William 'Bill' Heynes, had been Jaguar's chief engineer in the 1950s and now Jonathan Heynes, then aged 50, aimed to apply some of the thinking he'd learnt at the luxury carmaker to the Reliant Robin.

'We took the top twenty customer complaints from last year,' he said, 'and decided, in classic John Egan style [John Egan turned Jaguar round in the early 1980s before it was privatised from British Leyland], to hit those first! It's all small details that customers notice. And I want happy customers.' Such small details included a better cooling system, choke cable and an improved ashtray, but he also aimed to boost pride of ownership, with a new standard of lustrous clear-over-base paintwork – 'just like Jaguar uses':

You see, the Robin isn't as quiet as a Jaguar XJ6 ... but here's the sort of engineering problem I love. The challenge is to take 20kg of weight off the car by 'cuteness' of design, and then add it back as improved

Company owner Kevin Leech moved Reliant to this factory in Cannock, Staffordshire, alongside his Fletcher speedboats business.

During his brief spell in charge of Reliant, ex-Jaguar engineer Jonathan Heynes instigated the Robin Mk3, which was launched in 2000.

The Mk3 Robin had, apart from the doors, a total body redesign; here you can see the neat detail of its racing-car-style petrol cap surround.

Which other car to mug for the headlights on the Mk3? Why, they've been let loose in the Vauxhall stores and come out holding some lights from the Corsa hatchback.

Under the bonnet of the Mk3. The engine is, as ever, hard to get at, but battery and fluid intakes are easy to access.

sound-deadening, refinement and general 'better-ness'. I'm going right through the Robin and trying to lose, say, half a kilo from the starter motor, two-and-a-half from the engine, five from the chassis.

Indeed, a luxury Robin was soon built for Heynes' daily 40-mile commute, complete with leather upholstery, deep British Racing Green paint and gleaming spoked alloy wheels.

Heynes' efforts to restart engine production, overhaul the glass-fibre moulding process and get Reliant's potentially lucrative spare-parts business going were all chronicled in a fly-on-the-wall documentary for BBC2's *Trouble At The Top* series. It made compelling viewing. Heynes' South African wife, Samantha, was shown as the one-woman accounts department, handing out brown-paper wage packets to the sixty workers as the company got going again in hand-to-mouth fashion. Meanwhile, the boss himself outlined his plan to create a new Reliant sports car once Robin production was running smoothly.

He aimed to make fifteen three-wheelers a week at first, but by mid 1997 the weekly level was actually running at twenty-five. On the product front, Heynes launched a van version of the hatchback Robin and started work on completing a pickup model to join it, which had been initiated by Avonex but abandoned during their brief stewardship. He told me:

Reliant began by making vans anyway and I can see a ready market for a vehicle halfway in size between a courier's motorbike and a Suzuki van – with a 23ft turning circle it would be ideal for big cities like London. You see those three-wheeled Piaggio delivery trucks everywhere in France and Italy. So why not Reliant vans here?

The most unlikely customer you could possibly imagine, London's American Embassy, bought three Robin vans.

The interior of the Mk3 was all very familiar territory to Reliant veterans – very little was fundamentally different from the 1973 Robin, and none of it felt especially upmarket to the touch.

Reliant was just about keeping pace with contemporary aesthetics with its new Mk3, even though its potential market was rapidly and permanently dwindling.

The handsome visage of the Robin Mk3 masked a guilty secret: the car had not been submitted for certification, which the authorities did not take kindly to.

Jonathan Heynes, on the right, worked hard to turn Reliant round, but soon split from stakeholder Kevin Leech, for whom this Union Jack-bedecked Robin was built.

Ramshackle the plant may have seemed in the unforgiving light of BBC TV cameras, but Heynes was upbeat about his resources (he told me he'd uncovered £50,000 worth of serviceable design equipment underneath piles of old cardboard boxes) and unusually loyal staff:

> There's never been a problem with the staple product – the three-wheeler. It's a profitable car. As soon as you put four wheels on a Robin you're up against Metros, Clios, Cinquecentos and Skodas – a lot of good £7,000 cars. If you look at three-wheelers, there's no competition. I knew this was a business I could turn round.

For almost two years, stability and a realistic approach returned to Two Gates. However, the next bombshell was ready to drop towards the end of 1997.

Kevin Leech had become famous as the first billionaire resident of Jersey. He started out on his road to success by building his father's Manchester funeral parlour into a major chain of undertakers. Next, he invested in a medical research business, from which he became fabulously wealthy, choosing to then dabble in a mixed bag of ventures. He would become the seventeenth richest man in Britain, only to go spectacularly bankrupt in the bursting of the dot.com bubble in 2002. Back in 1997, he'd just made his latest purchase (to add to a portfolio that included Land's End and the Snowdonia mountain railway): Fletcher Speedboats. The Staffordshire boatbuilder was located at Burntwood, 14 miles away from Reliant.

Mr Leech now insisted that Reliant vacate the Two Gates site and move in with Fletcher Speedboats. As both cars and boats used glass fibre, there was plenty of logic to the scheme. Yet Jonathan Heynes was,

The interior of the patriotic Robin built for Kevin Leech (Jersey's most prominent billionaire before a spectacular bankruptcy), with red, white and blue seats and an enchanting pair of furry dice.

This gold-painted edition was launched at the end of 2000 to wave goodbye to the British legend, some sixty-five years after the Reliant name first appeared.

perhaps understandably, against it because Two Gates – Reliant's home since the late 1930s and where he was in total control – had more space and potential for his expansion plans. However, the partners couldn't agree and in 1998 Leech bought out the others. Heynes departed, no doubt bitterly disappointed and probably Reliant's best hope of a ground-up rebuild. In January 1999, Reliant finally quit its home of sixty-four years. The final fifty Robins built at Two Gates carried special plaques to commemorate their place in the company's history.

Heynes' legacy was also the upside to the upheaval: an almost totally restyled third-generation Robin was ready to go straight into production at the new Burntwood works. A modern, aerodynamic-looking nose now incorporated teardrop-shaped headlights from the Vauxhall Corsa, while the rear wheel arches had a rounded profile and even the fuel filler cap had been redesigned to give it the flavour of a racing car.

The work was undertaken by Andy Plumb, a graduate in automotive design from Coventry University, who was Reliant's chief designer for a year before moving on to greater things, including stints with Bentley, Nissan and MG. The designer of the original Robin, Tom Karen, would have been delighted to note that Andy's thorough makeover included removing the rain gutters, but he might have been mildly shocked that the interior he created in the early 1970s was largely unaltered, as was the entire chassis and drivetrain.

The three-car new Robin range started with the £8,137 LX, moved up to the £8,459 SLX, with its metallic paint and a radio/cassette, and was topped by the £9,654 BRG (for British Racing Green) or Royale (in blue), with fog lights, alloy wheels, luxury carpets and a medley of extra trim and chrome highlights. You could buy a brand new Peugeot 106 for almost a grand less than the LX. Yet in no way did this deter

The smartly finished interior of the Robin 65, with leather upholstery and a new steering wheel, plus an armrest between the two front seats.

Reliant addicts. By March 1999 there was a six-week waiting list and production was back at the now normal rate of thirty cars a week.

Reliant's turbulent past was behind it, an efficient new factory was up and running, a good-looking new design was on the market and customers were still, bafflingly to the mainstream world of motoring, clamouring for new Robins.

So how could it possibly be that in September 2000 company owner Kevin Leech – having sunk a reported £750,000 in the venture – announced that production of the Reliant Robin would soon end? He'd even had his own personal Robin sprayed with an enormous Union Jack paint job. The announcement dealt a hammer blow to everyone who'd stuck with the Reliant project through the tough times, from the workforce, many of whom had transferred from Two Gates, to the ever-faithful customers.

There were, it appears, two factors at play. First, Leech had acquired UK distribution rights to the French Ligier microcars range and the

Italian Piaggio compact commercial vehicles line-up. Reaction to these at the London Motor Show in 2000 had been very positive. The Reliant dealer network was especially positive towards the tiny Ligier cars because, as they were officially classed as 'quadricycles', they qualified for motorbike road tax (now £65 instead of £150) and licence stipulations, with the enormous benefit of possessing four wheels. Some 650 were sold in the first year of importation alone.

The second issue was much more controversial. According to Reliant authority John Wilson-Hall, whose fascinating book *Reliant Three-Wheelers: The Complete Story* was published in 2014, the so-called 'Robin 3' had gone on sale without anyone at Reliant bothering to ensure it was legal to use on the road.

All new designs of vehicle have to undergo tests to gain Type Approval from the Vehicle Certification Agency (VCA), which are designed to ensure they meet construction and safety laws. Low-volume vehicles can gain exception from some Type Approval rules, such as expensive crash tests, as the VCA has a mandate not to make it impossible for entrepreneurs to establish new-car building companies. Even so, all new designs of vehicle must be officially assessed so that, for example, lighting meets current standards. And, when all was said and done, the Reliant Robin hardly had a spotless reputation when it came to roadworthiness, now, did it?

The third-generation Robin had a substantially different body to the car it replaced, with, for instance, a much larger opening bonnet panel, but it apparently had never been submitted for inspection. Faced with an ultimatum that this was now mandatory, it seems Leech decided it simply wasn't worth the cost and uncertainties of the outcome. No more orders were taken after 30 November 2000.

On 14 February 2001, the production line finally, *finally*, ground to a halt. It had just completed the last of a run-out limited edition model called the Robin 65, rather mournfully celebrating six-and-a-half decades of Reliant manufacture with its gold paintwork, leather upholstery, walnut-dash panel, individual plaque with the owner's name engraved on it, and an eye-watering £10,000 price tag; at that time, you could purchase a four-wheeled, five-door, Malaysian-built Perodua Nippa economy car for much less than £5,000.

The very last car was bought by *The Sun* newspaper to give away in a reader competition. The winner was John Leigh of Weaverham, Cheshire, who correctly answered the none-too-taxing question: 'What was the colour of Del-Boy's motor?' It gave the paper the chance to

THE ROBIN IS BACK

■ Owners and lovers of the Robin will be pleased to know that this world famous car is now back in limited production.

■ The new BN-1 model has undergone extensive re-engineering with numerous design and detail changes.

RELIANT CARS LTD

■ Standard vehicle specifications include:-
• metallic paint • leather trim • alloy wheels • chrome instruments
...plus much more

new prices from £9995.00 (inc. VAT)

For all the facts write or call FREE today

0800 197 5664

Reliant Cars Ltd, FREEPOST MID 22177, Cannock, WS11 1BR

A press ad for the so-called BN-1 Robin, an abortive attempt to revive the car in the hands of a Suffolk entrepreneur.

publish a splash on 15 February crammed with 'lovely jubblys' and 'cushtys' cornily plucked from *Only Fools & Horses*. It was only the second new car John had ever owned, the first being a Hillman Avenger back in 1970, thanks to knowing the infamous Supervan was yellow. 'There goes a piece of British comic history,' the paper quoted actor David Jason, portrayer of Derek Trotter in the sitcom. 'It's a great day for road safety in Britain – let's hope the wind's not too strong on John's drive home,' it quoted comedian Bernard Manning, for editorial balance.

John Powell, proprietor of Michaels of Selby, was unperturbed by the Robin's demise. 'I see a bright future for us even if they stop making the three-wheelers. There are still 44,000 Reliants on the road in Britain, and owners are going to need spares for at least twenty years to come.' Another dealer, Pete Ricketts of MAC Motors in Tooting, south-west London, was more downbeat when I interviewed him for *Auto Express* magazine in 2000:

> The old faithfuls do keep coming back to us, but they're dying out ... I sell four or five secondhand ones a month – estates and vans are very popular. But I've had one new car in stock for 10 months and not sold it. I'm sure if they brought the price down we'd sell more. We've done our best with Reliants but now we sell scooters in a big way.

I also spoke to Mike Murphy, chairman of the 1,200-strong Reliant Owners' Club, and he expressed his dismay at the thought of the Robin finally heading into the sunset:

> My first reaction is that it's sad news if it means the end of Reliant as we know it. There's a strong following and people still want them. However, it's not a poor man's car any longer. It's got its quirks – it's no Ford Escort, after all – and it's very basic, but I think that's part of its attraction.

Almost unbelievably, there was yet one more attempt at a Robin resurrection. As if it were some giant, scuttling, motorised cockroach, the car simply would not be killed off. A man called Les Collier from Sudbury in Suffolk was so convinced that there was a good niche business to be had in continuing to make the Robin that his manufacturing company, B&N Plastics, agreed to pay £250,000 for the production rights. He got as far as organising a launch for the car before comprehending, just like Reliant itself, that he couldn't sell any unless the correct vehicle certification had been obtained.

Relations with Reliant, which had agreed to supply the mechanical parts, quickly turned acrimonious, and although the VCA certificates for the MkIII Robin were finally obtained on 21 December 2001, by then Collier had run out of money and was forced to sell his home to pay off his debt mountain. It really was the Robin's final, sad ending.

Since that time, though, the Robin has simply refused to go away, such is its permanent place stitched firmly into British motoring culture. Viewers of BBC2's *Top Gear* have been treated to several stunts and escapades in which the Robin is the fall guy. In these, it was rarely driven in the way that experienced owners would treat their cars and so, of course, it was easily wrong-footed, overturned and nearly destroyed for comic effect. Where the Robin wouldn't fit the stereotype of a petrol-powered clown, the *Top Gear* special effects department rigged it so it would. And why not? This was an entertainment show fronted by witty and slightly arrogant speed merchants, not a documentary series for earnest tricycle aficionados. Since leaving the BBC to make their own show, the three presenters have even bought some old Robins as runarounds for their new production company.

The shame of the Robin's media exposure, though, was to perpetuate the idea that Reliant Robins were unsafe. As Mike Murphy, former chairman of the Reliant Owners' Club, once said to me: 'It puzzles me when people say they're dangerous. If that was the case, then why is the insurance so much lower than for a four-wheeled car of the same value?'

And in 2011, just to add to the confounding nature of Britain's near-legendary three-wheeler, a data-crunching exercise by comparison website Confused.com revealed the Reliant Robin was, in fact, the safest car on the road in Britain. Fewer than 1 per cent of drivers had been involved in a collision in the previous five years, in stark contrast to the most crashed marque – Lexus – where more than 10 per cent of owners had made an insurance claim on their pranged motor cars.

Reliant Owners' Club treasurer Peter Huggins was quoted by the *Daily Mail* in 2011:

You have to drive them more carefully than a normal car and be more alert. They aren't unstable in corners if you don't take stupid risks or do what Jeremy Clarkson did and roll it over on a sharp bend … You get quite a few jokes about them but it's water off a duck's back.

Ten

Investigations and Investments

In previous chapters, we've journeyed together through the life and times of the Reliant Robin, saluting the earlier Regals and the short-lived Rialtos en route. We've squeezed ourselves into its Lilliputian front seats, been buffeted by juggernauts, bounced over every bit of road detritus that other vehicles throw into the middle of the carriageway, and withstood the jokes and jibes that these bizarre little vehicles have always elicited. We've also been able to celebrate their good points, including the ingenuity needed to make them legally compliant and their incredible ability to make a gallon of petrol go those many extra miles.

It will soon be two decades since the last new Robins were built. For years, though, their numbers have been reducing. From the Robin's introduction in 1973 via the Rialto interlude to the final three-wheeler being collected by its proud owner in 2001, the late Reliant expert Don Pither calculated that 63,055 examples were built. A combination of factors have colluded to give a probable survival rate of less than 10 per cent of that tally. MOT failures, crashed cars and other examples deemed simply too far-gone to be worthy of repair clearly account for most of the depletion. In its heyday, Reliant would have had you believe its cars were a breeze to work on, but that wasn't really the case and build quality was never more than passable at the best of times. Quite a few more cars have been deliberately broken up, hundreds for Robin/Rialto-only banger races on dirt tracks – which admittedly do make for entertaining viewing – and others to make use

Among the many indignities forced upon innocent Reliant three-wheelers by the producers of BBC2's *Top Gear* was this attempt to send one skywards.

of the chassis to turn them into American-style trikes with big wheels and a single seat.

People doing daft things with Robins could easily fill this book. It would begin with inappropriate replica Del Boy vans and extend to stretch limousines and rocket-powered Reliant-based dragsters. But for sheer carefree, three-wheeled fun, Ian Fuggle's story is hard to beat.

As a young graphic designer living in London in 1989, Ian and three friends decided to buy a Reliant each for the trip of a lifetime, a holiday in Monte Carlo:

> Mine was a P-reg Robin 850, which I painted as the Batmobile, while the others were a 750 Robin done up as a pirate ship and a Regal painted like the Mystery Mobile from *Scooby Doo*. We took them to the Reading Festival and, afterwards, nine of us set off straight to Monaco in the cars, via my mum's house in Deal.

Cruising through the French countryside, avoiding motorways, the convoy caused a huge stir in every village it passed through. 'We had

Monaco traffic police are none too amused with their three-wheeled invaders after Ian Fuggle's Robin stormed the principality.

kids on mopeds swarming around us everywhere. We were like Pied Pipers; people loved it.' After four days without a bed or a shower, they pulled into a campsite in Frejus and Ian met Tracy, who decided to hop on board for the final push down to the principality.

The reception, however, was a hostile one. Alerted by the skull-and-crossbones flag billowing from the Robin done up as a pirate ship, only Ian's car managed to cross the border (the pirate ship was turned away by police, the Mystery Mobile got lost in France anyway and Ian was escorted out with a police patrol car and outriders within hours). They were deemed undesirables, and so meandered their way back to Calais – and to disaster. Getting distracted for a moment, Ian trundled into the back of another (metal) car in the ferry queue and the *Scooby Doo* Regal smacked his Robin up the back.

The car was wrecked at about 10mph, just about managing to stagger back to Deal before a final trip to the scrapyard. But there was an upside: Ian and Tracy, and their two daughters, have been together ever since:

> The funny thing was, they were totally reliable all the way there and back, and mine was only running on three cylinders. I loved driving it. You had to slip into this tiny space, a bit like an aeroplane cockpit or a racing car seat, and it always felt very exciting. It was a great adventure.

Reliant three-wheelers cannot fail to become valuable classic cars. They're full of character and they tend to evoke a surge of nostalgia and delight in anyone who has grown up in the second half of the twentieth century.

The Reliant Owners' Club has, at the time of writing, almost 800 members, well down on its 1978 peak of almost 4,500 but still big enough to indicate that there is a solid nucleus of enthusiasm for the Robins and Rialtos that, somehow, have managed to elude the scrapyard, the heretic or the yobbo. If you own a Reliant, or want to own one, then you'd be mad not to join for advice, support and loads of ways to enjoy your car with likeminded souls (www.reliantownersclub.com).

I bought my 1992 Robin LX on the spur of the moment, partly motivated by not wanting to allow one more of this diminishing breed to be destroyed. I didn't take any advice, or even look at any other examples, and I will perhaps pay the price for being impulsive by finding I haven't exactly acquired the best example in the world.

The two Robins and a Regal gave Ian Fuggle and friends an odyssey across France that they would never forget; the cars proved surprisingly reliable on the mammoth trip.

But what about taking the plunge yourself? Existing owners are undoubtedly great sources of advice, as well as foreboding tellers of horror stories. I decided to speak to a couple of British specialists who were willing to share their knowledge and offer general guidance to anyone wet behind the ears when it comes to joining the three-wheeled brotherhood.

Joe Mason has become one of the UK's busiest Reliant specialists, with his Reliant Spares operation based in Cradley, on the Worcestershire/Herefordshire borders. Not only does he have a huge stock of the bits and pieces that many tentative and experienced owners will need to keep their cars on the road, but he also buys and sells Reliant-made vehicles – at least one a week and often sight-unseen over the phone – and usually has plenty of examples for sale. Joe recalls his introduction to the arcane world of their foibles and fables:

Before I started with Reliants I didn't know anything about them. I'm a biker, and I started to import classic Japanese motorbikes. I mostly used to find them in Italy, and it went very well for quite a long time. Then I had a big bike crash – smashed myself up in an accident. I spent weeks in hospital, then a year in a wheelchair, but in the end I made a 'miracle recovery', as they say, and pretty much got back to normal.

In his absence, the classic bike import business had fallen apart. Joe followed many other battle-scarred bikers and bought himself a Reliant Robin, with the intention to strip off the plastic body and turn the chassis into an American-style motor tricycle that wouldn't be so easy to fall off and yet would still give him, with a little imagination, the laid-back charm of a Harley-Davidson Trike.

'What amazed me was that when I advertised all the Reliant parts I didn't want, I sold absolutely everything instantly, every last nut and bolt,' Joe said, alerting him to the insatiable demand for everything to keep old Reliants going. He hasn't looked back:

There are certain things with these cars that you have to look out for. And the most important of these by far, something that I'll see on two out of every three cars I come across, are problems with the head gasket. When they go, you get oil and water mixing, and it's easy to know that there are issues if you see a yoghourt-y sort of pale gunk on the rocker cover. It's not easy to fix because the head gaskets aren't made any more, and anyway there's a very good chance that you'll ruin the engine if you try to take the head off. If you see this sign, it might be better to walk away.

This is a very expensive engine to rebuild. It's not like a good old BMC A-Series, where you can do a good job for under £1,000. New piston rings alone for the Reliant engine cost £300. We sell a lot of reconditioned engines for about £600 each, and it would cost you £1,200 or more to rebuild one yourself.

With the gearbox, if it jumps out of gear in first and reverse then there is definitely going to be wear in the gearbox, which will mean expensive rebuilding is needed. Avoid a whining back axle for the same reasons.

The next area for distress is rust in the chassis. This isn't an issue in cars from 1982 onwards, after the Rialto arrived, because the frames are galvanised, but the chassis of the early Robins can corrode badly. 'Even then,' said Joe, 'some years are a lot worse than others, for some unknown reason.'

The glass-fibre bodywork, of course, certainly cannot rust, but it's not immune to problems:

All glass-fibre can get micro blisters, whether the car is from the 1950s or one of the very last ones. You might need to grind it back if they're very bad and you want to get rid of them entirely. However, if you see spider-like chips in the paint surface, they're usually the result of the car having had an impact at some time. The odd thing is that they can emerge months after the accident happened. One of the very worst, most horrible, jobs is having to replace the door hinges. It would take two people a whole weekend to rectify. There should be a small strap, fitted at the factory, that stops the door from blowing open. If someone's removed that, probably to make the car easier to get into, then the hinges can get very weak from the extra strain put on them. The rubber window surrounds can also craze with age, and that is important because they hold the windows in place.

On the inside, Joe urges you to look for cracks in the dashboard, which could indicate more serious structural maladies. Also, if you can, to find a car with a black interior; pale trim, never the finest in quality terms, is usually peppered with stains and marks.

Originality is a noble intention for any classic car owner, but Reliants usually benefit from improvements. One worthwhile upgrade is to use adjustable shock absorbers at the back, which helps with both ride and stability. In the same vein, a wider track plants the car on the road better, but Joe recommended spacers behind each rear wheel to push the track out, rather than the more obvious fix of fitting wider wheels, as a better way to keep the car steering straight and true.

He also thought a few extra earths randomly around the car are a good way to keep the electrical system – a weakness on all cars with plastic bodies rather than steel – working well. There's also an electronic ignition module that replaces points and a condenser, at a cost of about £30, which will make the car much easier to live with either on a day-to-day basis or else for occasional weekend fun when you want the thing to fire up sweetly first time. Be warned: many of the replacement parts offered online, cautioned Joe, hail from China and have their own issues:

> Typically, they are copies that will fit okay but then not actually work very well. There's very little available in the way of genuine factory parts. It's a case of make do and mend, mostly. You need Mini or Land Rover suppliers for things like brake cylinders and master cylinders, and lights; a halogen conversion, by the way, is a really good idea.
>
> They are robust. Once set up right, they'll run and run.

However, well before you so much as slip the gearlever into first and pull away, there is one very important aspect of re-commissioning a

Robin or Rialto that hasn't been driven for a long time, and that's the fuel lines that carry petrol from the tank at the back to the carburettors at the front:

> You really do need to make sure, before you start the engine up, that you've changed the fuel line for a modern one. The problem is modern petrol; since the cars were new, petrol has had more and more ethylene added. That might be good for the environment and everything, much greener, but the ethylene in modern petrol kills the fuel lines. There are a few corner sections and links that are made of rubber, less than six inches length in total, and the ethylene turns these sections to jelly. They split very quickly, and it's crucial that that doesn't happen, or else you run the risk of an engine fire, and the whole car could go up in flames almost immediately. It's one of the most important issues to be aware of.

As with most things that rely on expertise, it's always a good idea to get a second opinion. For this, I was fortunate to be able to talk to Ken Akrill at Keygate Motors in Chatham, Kent.

I made the journey to the company, tucked away in a yard accessed through an arch under the A2 flyover, to discover a small but valuable seam of Reliant experience. The garage used to sell the cars new and Ken, who is the workshop manager and general parts guru, has worked there for some forty-five years. In fact, I was gladdened to find him probing the innards of a very original-looking (i.e. tired) Rialto estate when I called round to buy a new replacement ignition barrel, petrol cap and boot lock for my own Robin LX – all of which he was somehow able to pull from darkened corners of the premises.

'We're always happy to give people advice about the cars,' Ken said. 'And I suppose there isn't much I don't know about them':

> I think that the main issue, for anyone looking to buy a car for themselves, is to find one that simply has a current MOT. It doesn't matter what the car looks like or how good the condition of the engine appears but, if it has an MOT, then you absolutely know that it's sorted and running on all four cylinders.

Ken concurred that the head gasket is a weak spot on the Reliant engine. But all is not lost on replacements:

They do have an issue with this, the oil and water mixing, but you can get replacements, if you know where to look. The thing is, all parts for these cars are getting scarcer and scarcer. Often it depends on what's left in stock. It is possible to get batches of new parts made, of course, but companies won't make a new batch of *anything* unless there's a good chance that they'll sell them all, or at least most of them.

Ken declared that engine rebuilds, at least from his point of view, simply weren't economic any longer. 'We don't do them any more,' he said flatly, echoing Joe Mason's view.

'You've got to watch the kingpin on the front wheel and steering box. If it wobbles then it's shot,' Ken added. 'And the electrics, well, they're all right. They're pretty basic, unlike a modern car. Everything is fused':

There definitely used to be a stigma about them, but they're actually great fun. As an investment, I'd go for one of the last Mk3s. They're very hard to find now, but it's definitely the best of the lot.

That might well be the case if you want the most efficient, least decrepit Robin. But in my opinion, it's the first series of cars made between 1974 and 1981 – hamstrung as they all are with rust-prone chassis – that are likely to be the ones that really will, one day, command big sums as cult collectibles, following the earlier Bond Bug into five-figure values.

It's only these early Robins that have the original Ogle Design styling, the one-piece glass hatchback, the delectable smoothness of a gutter-free roof, the cheekiness of two round headlights in a snub-nosed frontage and a colour palette rich in browns, greens, golds, yellows, oranges and purples for both paintwork and interior trim that gives off the authentic aroma of genuine 1970s kitsch. No doubt about it, the undiluted British 1970s 'tat factor' of the Robin is very much intrinsic to its esoteric charm, and the oldest ones have that in spades. If you get all misty for the days when you sat in front of the telly in your flares and kipper tie, watching *Man About The House* and tucking into a Vesta curry, then you'll find a Reliant Robin simply oozes period charm. Or, indeed, you might just fancy one because, once you get it back in decent mechanical health, it's a laugh to own and drive and gets you more stares, grins and pointing fingers than any Lamborghini or Aston Martin.

'Very late cars … the Mk3, is probably the best,' said Joe Mason:

They were only made in 2000 and 2001, so they're rare. You'll pay £3,000 for a 60,000-mile car and £6,000 for a 30,000-mile car. But values of the earlier cars are leaping ahead. They are a great investment, as they just keep going up and up, and there are very few in really good condition. They do exist but they never come up; the good ones never reach the open market. It might now mean £5,000 for a fantastic one, if you could find such a thing.

Just look at what has happened to the Bond Bug. Pretty soon, a good one of those is going to be worth £10–12,000. One day, it'll be a £25,000 car. I mean, the Robin is bound to go the same way in the end. It's got three wheels and it's British. How mad is that?

Bibliography

Lockton, Daniel, *Rebel Without Applause: Volume 1, From Inception To Zenith* (Bookmarque, 2003)
Marshall, Tony, *Microcars* (Sutton Pubishing, 1999)
Payne, Elvis, *The Reliant Motor Company* (Nostalgia Road Publications, 2016)
Pither, Don, *Reliant Regal & Robin* (Sutton Publishing, 2001)
Rees, Chris, *Three-Wheelers A-Z: The Definitive Encyclopaedia of Three-wheeled Vehicles from 1940 to Date* (Quiller, 2014)
Wilson-Hall, John, *Reliant Three-Wheelers: The Complete Story* (Crowood Press, 2014)
Wotherspoon, Nick, *'Lawrie' Bond: The Man And The Marque* (Bookmarque, 1993)

The Reliant world abounds with replicas of the 'Del Boy' Supervan; indeed, several different examples were used throughout the filming of the show between 1981 and 2003.